Advance Praise For
Habits Don't Lie!

In this masterpiece, Michael shares with us the missing link to enduring greatness - Responsibility. He has masterfully shown us in "Habits Don't Lie" that it's not enough to focus above the surface of the proverbial Iceberg (Skill, talent, education, etc.) but, with diamond-like characteristics has unveiled to us the habits that will point us to grit, resilience, responsibility, consistency, AND Trust while one is persistently under pressure. This is a definite MUST read for business and life.
- Dr Ray Charles, Best Selling Author, Enough IS Enough

I am astonished by Michael's attention to detail, recapitulating the poignant times and rewards of his life lessons. "Habits Don't Lie" delivers an unadulterated realism with candid and authentic narratives that will intrigue, motivate and support every reader. Crafted creatively, seven practical and powerful steps towards healing, self-mastery and most importantly.... living your very best life. "Habits Don't Lie" will be your best investment in the world's greatest asset.... You!
-Shawan L. Dortch, BBA, MAT, Founder, H.E.A.R.D Humanitarian Corporation

"Habits Don't Lie!" is one of those books that you want to read over and over again every year to make sure you're staying on course. Michael's stories are engaging and full of teachable moments. This book will motivate you to challenge your obstacles and look at things in a new way ... a way that will help you WIN.
-Vickie Gould, Law of Attraction Business and Book Coach

I was moved reading "Habits Don't lie". While I was not surprised that Michael Wynn lives by a code - the stories he weaves that helped develop that code are powerful! I worked with (or was it for) Michael for years and had no idea about the struggles that gave him the strength and confidence that he exudes. The book is about family, love, determination and success. Join the spiritual Journey as you open the first page and prepare yourself to Target Success!
-Eleanor A. Harris, Ph.D.

I was truly motivated by this book's honesty, compassion and insight. Michael's personal anecdotes and perseverance are truly encouraging.... You will find yourself incorporating these life-changing habits in your daily life. "An inspirational masterpiece" ....
-Bobby Stinnette Licensed Professional Counselor B A New You Counseling and Wellness Center

Michael Wynn took the hand he was dealt, sorted his cards and discovered his gifts. More importantly, he used his gifts to achieve success and coaches' others to do the same. His story is compelling, soul stirring, inspiring, and a roadmap for success.
- Irma Givens, Daughters of Detroit, LLC, College Instructor, Speaker, Communications Coach and Author of "Your Crazy is Making Me Crazy"

This book presented by Mr. Michael Wynn is an eye opener, experiencing obstacles develop our character; however, we must never give up on our dreams and aspirations. I encourage the younger generation to read this book. Semper Fi
-Cedric L. Knott, Ph.D., CFE

I was completely thrilled to have a book that shines a light on the positive side of habit. I was able to directly relate to the personal stories…..I'll be referring back to this book for the habit tips for sure.
-Jamel Randall RYT, LMT
Owner of The Trap Yoga + Massage Studio

HABITS DON'T LIE!

7 Habits to Overcome Obstacles to Win

Michael D. Wynn

Copyright © 2018 Michael D. Wynn All rights reserved.

This book or parts thereof may not be reproduced in any form, stored in any retrieval system, or transmitted in any form by any means—electronic, mechanical, photocopy, recording, or otherwise—without prior written permission of the author or publisher, except as provided by United States of America copyright law. You may email the author at: mikewynn@coachwin.com

Disclaimer: In no way is this book intended to diagnose, treat, cure, or provide preventive advice on medical care or to prevent any disease. In this book, I share my personal experiences and give my opinions on how I overcame obstacles and my disorder. However; this book is not intended to provide any medical advice, and I highly recommend that anyone seeking medical options should consult their doctor or licensed medical expert, not this book.

The information, testimonials, and examples used herein are not intended to represent or guarantee that anyone will achieve the same or similar results. Each individual's success depends on many factors, including his or her background, follow-through, action, dedication, desire, and motivation. Visit the author's website at: https://www.coachwin.com

Cover by: Michael Corvin

~ Dedication ~

To My Mother Flora Jean
You are truly missed, and never forgotten.

To My Brother Sandy
Your protection to us never went unnoticed.

To My Sister Sharon
The gleam of your sunshiny smile still brings me joy.

To My Father Bernard
I will always honor our "Win" family connection.

If you can't fly then run, if you can't run then walk, if you can't walk then crawl, but whatever you do, you have to keep moving forward."

~Martin Luther King Jr.

Contents

Acknowledgments	11
Foreword - Norma T. Hollis	13
Introduction - Crazy, Lost, and Broken; I Was	15
Chapter 1- Remembering Moments	23
Chapter 2- The Choices We Have	48
Chapter 3- In Search for a Fixed Mindset	77
Chapter 4- But, Habits Don't Lie	103
Chapter 5- Habit One: "Visualize Faith"	124
Chapter 6- Habit Two: "Be Real"	134
Chapter 7- Habit Three: "Target Success"	143
Chapter 8- Habit Four: "Know Money"	152
Chapter 9- Habit Five: "Live Health"	167
Chapter 10- Habit Six: "Just Win"	178
Chapter 11- Habit Seven: "Think Repeat"	186
Conclusion: Demonstrate Your Win!	195
About the Author	199

Acknowledgments

When I first decided to write this book, I received tremendous support from my family. I am truly blessed to have the Wynn family and the Holloway family's love and support during my journey to write this book. Special thanks to my siblings Calvin, Fredrick, Charlette, and Gregory; and my children Michael Jr., Patrick, and Lynette for allowing me to be open and transparent with my voice in telling the stories that supported my victory. To my niece Riel and my nephew Otis Jr. who always gave me the reflections of their mother, my sister Sharon, as I saw through them, her caring and comforting spirit gave me the motivation to tell my story. And special thanks to my daughter Leslie Hardy who provided me with some well-balanced critiques throughout this book.

When it comes to my friends, I can often count on their support; as I ask, I will receive, and with many times a "yes" came before knowing what was asked of them. I would like to thank those who read early versions of my book, like Stratford and Patricia Johnson, Rene Richardson, and Dana Billings, which were all a value to me for proof-reading this book.

When a professional touch is necessary, you need the best, and I was truly blessed to connect with some of the best people on Planet Earth! I thank you, Norma Hollis, for teaching me how to use my authentic voice in every situation as a tool for execution. Thank you, Pam Perry, ` for being the PR coach who is always working hard with a smile and showing your true passion for social media and marketing. Especially, the support that was provided to me to get my book shown and talked about in one of the articles in your Speaker Magazine in the April 2018 issue that was displayed at the Les Brown Power Voice conference. To my book coach Vickie Gould, I thank you for providing me with a successful road map, a unique writer program, the opportunity to write a bestselling book, and the insight you gave to create a book that would help people advance their personal and business lives. Wow; and having a "Gladiator" on your team like my editor Andrea McMurry, made a huge difference for me to tell my story so that it is clearly heard around the world. I thank you, Andrea, for always being armed with your sword, ready to slay any unnecessary words. The wrong use of a word or a thought that is not clear which might block me from telling my story the way it should be told.

Now, as it comes to love, I could not imagine attempting to write this book without the love and support that I always receive from my wife Joyce for anything that I do. She kept me in my routine with writing, she cheered me on through my writer's block, she comforted me with words of praise through the uncomfortable situations that I knew had to be told in this book. The love we share is everlasting, and I know my loving wife will always be by my side for the success we build together.

Foreword

About 15 years ago, I offered one of my speaking training events in my hometown of Detroit, MI. My company, Speakers Etcetera was based in Los Angeles, CA, and I was on a multi-city tour to conduct a speaking series: *Command Attention, The Process to Become a Professional Speaker.* This fall event was held on the Focus Hope campus in a beautiful, historical building that attracted many people who were looking to develop or improve their speaking skills. As I watched and listened to the many introductions, I heard the excitement, desire, and passion of many who spoke about helping others.

I remember speaking with Michael Wynn on the telephone about the training, and after meeting him, it did not take long to see why he made the investment. As one of the people who talked about his passion in helping others, Michael also talked about his financial background as an auditor, and financial literacy trainer. He volunteers many hours speaking and training through the Accounting Aid Society and wanted his message to be clear and concise.

Well, Michael was one of my favorite clients who traveled to many of my trainings in Los Angeles and Dallas, as well as other events in Detroit. As my company grew, I added a focus on Authenticity with opportunities to find your authentic voice. Michael took advantage of the opportunity to become an Authenticity Coach and Speaker. Through the process of using his authentic voice, Michael brings awareness, integrity, motivation and inspiration to his business as he speaks and coaches' individuals, groups, business teams, youth, college students, and others. So, when I heard that he was writing a book, I knew it would reflect his authenticity and his transparency in expressing the trials and tribulations he has experienced and learned from.

What I see in *Habits Don't Lie* is Michael's way of reaching out to others by sharing and honoring his gifts. He had obstacles and breakthroughs that led him to discover that habits indeed do not lie. Through this book, Michael strongly believes that these life-changing habits are the formula to helping others. In this book, Michael is serving many in this world, and I am honored to have an everlasting friendship with him. I recommend that you prepare yourself to gain a deep understanding of what Michael is willing to expose to the world about who he was and who he is now through his breakthrough.

Good Reading,

Norma T. Hollis
America's Leading Authenticity Expert

Introduction

Crazy, Lost, and Broken; I was

I am so pleased to be in this space to share and discuss some amazing experiences that I went through that may help you and many others overcome obstacles to achieve your breakthrough and elevate success. I thank you for selecting *Habits Don't Lie*, and I hope that you will find something in this book that will personally help you to become more successful in your personal and business life. This book is about how ordinary people can use certain habits to become extraordinary by overcoming obstacles for a breakthrough. *Habits Don't Lie* speaks to the necessary laser-focus habits that one should have, especially after a setback. Through my journey in this book, I will discuss the purposeful and life-changing habits I formed from childhood to manhood to help deal with my difficult circumstances and dark days. I hope that my experience with recovery, through the pain and tears, will help many people recognize how to deal with overcoming their obstacles, especially men like me who were taught to tough it out and not to show their true emotions.

You will get a peek at the opportunities and advantages that I had over and over through my formal years of education, college, and employment. I often found a way to accomplish many of my goals and ambitions, but at other points I took on too many tasks and lost balance. As a financial auditor, accountant, fraud examiner, and financial literacy trainer, I was fortunate to find great employment with my qualifications and skills. Yet, I also had the deep desire to be an entrepreneur, so I tried my hand at several business opportunities, including running a specialty-marketing retail business, becoming a landlord for rental property, investing in real-estate, and training to be a licensed builder. I later found a passion to become a speaker, as a life and business coach.

Overall, I found my niche and used it to consult, coach, and speak with individuals and organizations about how to use successful habits to overcome obstacles and grow their businesses. Using the habits that I wrote about in this book paid off for me. I am doing well now, and I am truly blessed to live a life of happiness and abundance with my loving wife Joyce and our blended families in our beautiful home in Metro Detroit. However, life was not always easy or abundant. As difficult as it is for me to tell my story, this book reflects the ebbs and flows in my life; destructive thinking, as well as unusual and unwanted behaviors became obstacles and distractions in my life, for which I had to find a critical and consistent solution.

Not to offend anyone or be part of a stigma, but I describe one of my biggest obstacles as being "Crazy," since I strongly felt that way. I had no desire to sleep, I worked like time was running out for me, and I had

Introduction: Crazy, Lost, and Broken; I Was

feelings of hopelessness. I was diagnosed with the mental conditions of depression and bipolar disorder. Before I knew any better, I was convinced that I had to indulge in a series of drugs that I called my LPD nightmare. I had an on-and-off relationship with the drugs Lithium, Prozac, and Depakote that required me to constantly adjust to how my body felt. But, it is finally time for me to come out of hiding from the sense of shame I felt about myself. I need to tell how I defeated a potentially long-term disorder that might have overcome me had I not taken charge. I'm sure that by telling my story, I will help others to either face what they are dealing with or feel comfortable enough to share their story about the obstacles they face.

Although, I talk about how I rebounded to success from my "Crazy," I was also "Lost" and "Broken" from the passing away of three family members all within three years. My healthy mother lost her life after an unexpected illness. My older brother, a ranked black-belt instructor, passed away from an emergency-room medical error, and my sister, who was a critical-care nurse, committed suicide due to her mental illness. To make matters even worse, I suffered loss from a divorce after 27 years of marriage, then had to deal with a devastating financial loss and bankruptcy, while my youngest child was on her journey to become a doctor. Overcoming my disorder and the challenges that came through dealing with the losses took a toll on my health and broke down my spirit. Yet, I fought not to let the disorder that I overcame return. As I embraced the habits that I learned to get through my obstacles, I had to fight hard to avoid a relapse, so I would not become a victim again to that ugly disorder. I had to be determined to really embrace those habits that got me through.

My journey did come with some happiness, and this book will describe how I found habits to use consistently for my medical and financial recovery. I give the glory and praises to God; it is so wonderful to feel stronger, more resilient, happy, and alive. I am truly blessed to still be in the right state of mind, with a better connection with my sons Mike Jr. and Patrick, and my daughter Lynette. Now, after 13 years of overcoming my disorder, it is an honor for my sons, my family, and me to celebrate Lynette's accomplishments as a doctor. In May 2018, she graduated from the University of Michigan medical school, and Dr. Lynette Wynn is now training as an OB/GYN at Morehouse School of Medicine in Atlanta

I hope to share in detail the habits that I used to turn my obstacles into wins. Allow me to be transparent; I realized that these simple habits would change my way of thinking because of the success of my recovery. I was motivated to use a practical approach for balance, and by implementing these habits to transform myself, I was able to grow out of a depressed state of mind. One of the many discussions with my mother was about habits. She had a lot of insight to tell me that my habits don't lie because I can grow to become successful by implementing good habits. However, I can also fall just as easily by making bad choices or using bad habits. As I grew older and wiser through my trials and tribulations, I finally got it! *Habits Don't Lie!*

I hope this book will motivate you to challenge your obstacles by using these life-changing habits. These habits may raise some issues, provide insights, and give recommendations for you to personally deal with obstacles and become more resilient for a win.

Habit One: VISUALIZE FAITH reminds us about the importance of daily prayer and meditation to seek mental relaxation and freedom that will reach far beyond any material existence. New discoveries, lessons learned from experts on faith, and confidence provided me with tools that helped me defeat my depression and bipolar disorder. The Visualize Faith habit guides you towards the victories that will make you feel more positive, less fearful, and unstoppable by allowing you to transform into a life of accepting faith, as your memories live on.

Habit Two: BE REAL examines authenticity by encouraging you to live an authentic life from the moment you wake up. This habit was, and still is, part of my daily routine to overcome my obstacles and learn to make peace with myself and others; to forgive and go forward. Be Real allows you to accept your intuitions through self-communication, as you incorporate abundance, feel good about your integrity, and inspire others as you lead by example.

Habit Three: TARGET SUCCESS will help you identify your purpose, passion, and accountability to create a driving desire and to achieve your goals and objectives with energy. The Target Success habit sometimes means saying "No," to the good, so you can say "Yes," to the best. This habit is the action plan to organize your time, utilize personal and business systems, depend on resources, take up daily reading, and find greatness through personal development. The Target Success habit will also help you create time-management controls, identify powerful personal and business relationships, and secure a connection with a mastermind or accountability group to evaluate and bring success to immense fulfillment.

Habit Four: KNOW MONEY identifies how we should look at financial literacy as a life mission and to understand and take control over our financial cycles. Even when demoralized from a financial disaster or recovering from bankruptcy, this habit will help you understand the value of financial stability. The Know Money habit also provides insight for starting or completing a home and business growth plan for multiple streams of income, eliminating debt, and controlling impulse spending. This habit will help you to recognize the importance of a financial-net wellness plan to develop a living legacy.

Habit Five: LIVE HEALTH examines the importance of understanding that your body is a temple and recognizing the need to stay healthy, before there is a health crisis for a preventable health condition. The Live Health habit encourages you to be in true health-wellness and fitness-obedience with your doctors, dentists, and other health specialists. This habit also guides you to your health greatness as you feed the brain, build and fuel the body, nurture your spirit, and learn how to pamper yourself and laugh again.

Habit Six: JUST WIN expresses focusing on your passions, thinking positive, accepting the commitment, and surrounding yourself with the right people who have the right attitude. The Just Win habit helped me recognize how to celebrate my small wins. This perspective allowed me to draw the connection of my last name and my "Winn-Wynn" attitude. The Just Win habit provides a bold and exciting perspective on what it means to create a mindset of "No Excuses, No Blame," in order to achieve the results that you need to overcome obstacles. It enables you to eradicate destructive thinking, and to rid toxic people from your life. This habit will also help you feel energized, motivated, and inspired to win at achieving your goals.

Habit Seven: THINK REPEAT shows the importance of a do-over, the glory of a second chance, or a repetition for clarity. The habit also focuses on the importance of journaling your daily thoughts, dreams, goals, and objectives. As you learn to log your money, food, and health habits for comparison data, financial growth and health-wellness are inevitable. This habit sets the standards to redo, readjust, then rejoice.

Here is what I ask from you, incorporate these habits in your life; celebrate and share the small and big wins that come as a breakthrough for your transformation. Please follow up with Coach "Win", LLC at: https://www.coachwin.com for more information on services and special offers to support you through your habit success and journey to greatness!

Michael D. Wynn

"The starting point for both success and happiness is a healthy self-image."

~Dr. Joyce Brothers

Remembering Moments

A Growing Self-Image

Growing up, as I watched my mother care for my family, I recognized that habits could be a powerful tool to have. To understand who I am and my journey as the third oldest of seven children, five boys and two girls, you need to know and understand the politics of a big family.

Being part of my family was hard for me, since I *was* the favorite child, at least that is what I had to keep reminding my siblings since I was named after "Michael," the angel from heaven. Although Mama would often tell us, "Each one of you is my favorite child," I'm sure she had to say that to keep my siblings emotionally balanced. As you can see, we had plenty of fun.

Life was not all that bad growing up in a family with a low-income status. Although many people would call us "poor," that never stopped us from having fun, because we lived in a happy, clean household that was very rich in spirit. In fact, as children, we never knew what poor was until we got older. From the age of four years old, I lived on the northeast side of Detroit on Clairmont, down the street from our grandmother, who we called 'Mama Hushie.' Mama Hushie, one of six girls from a small town called Star City, Arkansas, was a stern lady who didn't put up with any mess.

My parents had many struggles raising a large family. To help make ends meet, Mama had to get a job as a cashier

Chapter 1: Remembering Moments

at the King Cole Super Market located a couple blocks from home, although her passion was to be a stay-at-home mom, watching and caring for her children as they grew up. Since we stayed just down the street from Mama Hushie, we had to spend the day with her when Mama was at work.

I was an active and happy kid who expected a lot of attention. Even as a child, I had to create some drama just to be in the middle of the action. When we played in Mama Hushie's backyard under the berry bushes and pear trees, I climbed my way up to the top of the second-story stairs, located at the back of the house. There I claimed my space as the 'King,' daring anyone to dethrone me, or push me off the 4 x 4-foot landing where I stood, as I held my arms up into the sky yelling, "I am the King!" As the 'Great Ruler,' the only defense I had was my 'Loyal Subject,' Mama Hushie, who I begged to save me whenever my brothers tried to push me off the landing or put their hands on me. My outcry usually got them in trouble, and they had to go and answer to her, while I had time to reclaim the 'throne' and my kingship.

Each afternoon, we had to wait at Mama Hushie's house until Mama got home. I knew when Mama got off work, so I sneaked into the living room just to see her through the big bay window, walking down the street towards the house in her King Cole uniform, with bags in her hands. The sight of Mama was exciting for me, because her self-image and pride always shone from her face, no matter what. Since we didn't have a car, we had to take the bus or Mama Hushie had to drive us around if we had to go far. Because of this lack, we always had to get up very early for church or spend a lot of time with Mama Hushie during her shopping sprees at her favorite spots in Hamtramck, a Polish community where she loved to shop.

I remember when we moved from Clairmont to Martindale Street on the Northwest side of Detroit. There were days when I saw my father, who worked for the City of Detroit in the Department of Public Works as a "garbage man," coming home in stained overalls after his work day. Although my father did not have much time to play with us one-on-one, I was still happy to see him come home after a long day of working overtime. My father got a ride home from his co-worker, who dropped him off in the garbage truck that was used for the day. Sometimes, while playing outside with my friends, I saw the big white garbage truck pull up in front of the house, then stop. My father would climb down out of the truck and wave at me and my friends before he went into the house.

The neighborhood kids sometimes teased me about my dad being a garbage man. My dad, who had so much pride in having a job, told me, "Son, this is why you work hard, so people can talk about you," as he smiled with a little laughter. Then he said, "You should not worry about what people say. A job is a job, and you should always have one." I really respected my father's advice about not worrying over what kind of job to have, but just the importance having one. I visualized starting with a small job and growing it into something bigger with more opportunities. This dream became so real to me; I could only grow in my thinking to keep trying and developing more.

When I was six, I noticed for the first time my mama was pregnant, carrying my sister Charlette. My brothers,

Chapter 1: Remembering Moments

Sandy, Calvin, Fredrick, and I, were so excited about having a little sister. After Charlette was born, my mother became a stay-at-home mom again. The joys of a new baby in the household gave me and my brothers the opportunity to fuss over our sister. I also got to be Mama's number-one helper after Charlette was born. One time she asked me to go the store with her, without my siblings, and I felt really special.

A walk to the supermarket or local hardware store required us to get out the two-wheeled folding shopping cart and the shopping list. During any such outing, Mama always reminded us about her expectations for our behavior, manners, and patience. Mama, staying on point, said, "Your habits show who you are; they don't lie. So, if you practice good habits then you will be good; otherwise the bad habits will keep you in trouble." Since I was so excited about just being out, I nodded my head like I was really listening. However, I actually missed out on what she meant about habits. I blatantly ignored a nugget of wisdom that she expressed to me.

After getting to the supermarket and walking up and down the wide aisles, avoiding the wet floors near the yellow caution signs, my excitement really began to show. I pushed the shopping cart, bobbing my head like I was doing the shopping, as I checked out my favorite junk foods lined down both sides of the aisle. I saw Frosted Flakes cereal, Captain Crunch, Jif peanut butter, Nilla wafers, Oreo cookies, Chunky and Milky Way candy bars, as well as some of those orange slice candies that Mama Hushie always had in her house. I thought to myself, "I can't wait to get my treat for helping Mama." I continued to follow Mama around the store, dropping hints. I watched her go over her grocery list to make sure she didn't forget anything, and I thought this would be the best time to ask her for a Chunky bar. But Mama said, "No, not today, because I'm going to make some dessert tonight."

I remember getting very quiet inside, trying not to hear "No," especially since I felt like I *should* get a reward. So, when Mama spoke to the cashier and looked away, I stuck the candy in my shirt pocket. Feeling entitled, yet somewhat guilty at the same time, I gripped the candy bar and held onto it, with my right hand crossed over my chest to the left side of my shirt pocket. I acted like Mama was unaware of this candy, as I tried to help her load the bags into the shopping cart using only my left hand, lifting one bag at a time.

I just *knew* I had gotten away with something, but shortly after we got home, Mama asked me to take the bags in the house, then come and explain what was in my shirt pocket. Looking confused, I wasn't sure what to say, so I lied right away, "The man in the store said it was okay."

Mama replied, "What man? And why would he say it's okay to steal?"

Still holding onto my pocket, I started tearing up and said, "I don't know. Because I was being good, I think."

Mama glared at me with an angry look on her face and said, "Boy, be truthful."

Before she could start the next sentence, I said, "But Mama, I was really being good. How come I couldn't have a treat?

Chapter 1: Remembering Moments

She looked at me and said, "Because I said so. But you would lie to me and steal a candy bar to make matters even worse!"

I cried a little to show my sorrow and remorse, thinking maybe there was a chance of getting out of a whipping. Well, that acting scene was not convincing enough because when Mama started lecturing about her disappointment, I knew it was a done deal. I was going to get a whipping.

While standing there in dread of the punishment, I watched Mama sit down in one of the brown chairs in the living room and start to put on her shoes. Not knowing what to say, I stood in silence, watching her. When she finished, she stood and said, "Let's go." She walked to the door and yelled at my oldest brother Sandy that we were going back to the store. It was the most uncomfortable time I ever spent with Mama, as we walked all the way back to the supermarket, a couple blocks away. That day, however, the walk seemed like a mile, as I watched the sweat run down the side of Mama's face and studied her look of disappointment. She never said a word while we walked back to the store.

Once we got to the supermarket again, I saw her beautiful and polite spirit appear, the one she always preached about to us, saying that we should put on our best regardless. She calmly asked for the store manager. I just remember being scared and embarrassed as she explained to him that I took a candy bar without paying for it, that there would be no stealing in her family, and that her son had something to say. I just stood there, thinking, "If I get out of this alive, I will never steal again."

Mama then said, in a stern tone, "Michael, what do you have to say about that candy bar?" I looked up at that tall, slim man, wearing a green-striped apron, as he waited patiently. I remorsefully said, "I just want to say I am sorry for stealing the candy bar and making my mama mad at me for stealing. I will never do anything like this again."

Well, not only did Mama make me give the candy bar back, she told the store manager that I would work for him the following two weekends cleaning up around the store with no pay. However, the store manager replied, "That is a nice gesture but, because of his age, the store policy won't allow him to work at the store even if it is for free."

So instead, Mama made me write a letter of apology, that I had to read to Mama Hushie, before giving it to the store manager. Once we arrived back home, I tried to sneak in without talking to my brothers, but Mama called me into the kitchen. As I walked in, I pushed the swinging door closed, so my brothers could not hear us talking. Mama said to me, "I need you to help me put these groceries up," and she started lecturing me again, reminding me about the spanking that I was going to get.

After I was done putting away the groceries, I tried to slip out of the kitchen unseen, but Sandy, who was eavesdropping, just had to say while laughing, "Hey my brother, do you think ya still the favorite? Too bad daddy is not here to give you one of his short and quick whippings. You got Mama, and she's going to tear you up!" And that's exactly what she did.

Chapter 1: Remembering Moments

After I got my whipping, and right before bedtime, I still felt like I had really disappointed Mama. I looked in her room and saw her lying down in bed with both nightstand lights on, as she read her Bible. Before I could say anything, just like Mama, she gave me some words of comfort, and reminded me why I got that spanking. She then explained the importance of learning my lesson, because she refused to have a crook or thief living under her roof. She told me to hold my head up, and to work on forgiving, forgetting, and moving forward to heal as fast as I could. She quoted a verse from the Bible, like she always did to prove her point. She made me read from Colossians 3:13, as my voice cracked, "Bear with each other and forgive one another, if any of you has a grievance against someone. Forgive as the Lord forgave you." After I finished reading, we said a prayer and I felt a sense of relief. I cherished that moment, because Mama always told us about having a visual of faith with a can-do-better spirit. Feeling her forgiveness gave me a great moment of knowing that I had another chance to prove my honesty and my love to her in return. This moment instilled in me a habit to "Visualize Faith," which reminded me of the importance of daily prayer and meditation to seek mental relaxation and freedom that reaches far beyond any material existence.

While still in elementary school, I remember moving again, this time to Ohio Street where we planted our roots, at least until I finished high school. My sister Sharon was born soon after we moved, and my youngest brother Gregory followed two years later. It seemed like everything in this neighborhood was just too close for comfort; it was hard to have any real fun without getting in trouble. We lived down the street from a convent where the nuns of St. Brigid Roman Catholic Church served. We went to school about four blocks away at Courtis Elementary. My father transferred to the Davidson Yard, which was a block away from the school, and Mama decided to go back to work, so she took a job at our school in the lunch room. The kids at school loved Mama, who always had that same beautiful smile, and they called her the "Lunchroom Lady." However, the teachers and staff called her Mrs. Wynn, and they were ready to report to her if any of us acted up.

The neighborhood was changing as more black families moved in, but it was still very integrated with white and black families. We had some great, fun white neighbors who lived on our block; however, we also had some hateful and not-so-friendly neighbors who lived behind us, across the alley. Mama was the most authentic person I knew because she always faced reality, even with boundaries. She taught us not to judge people based on the way they looked, especially by the color of their skin. As kids, however, we sometimes fell short in defending ourselves from people using racially-motivated words towards us, thinking that most people we crossed were good people who were just being funny.

Well, Mama corrected that thought quickly, during the winter of 1965, about a year after we moved in. My brother Calvin and I often played outside in the snow in the backyard where there was a chain-link fence that separated our yard from the alley. We made snow angels and sometimes a crooked snowman, who was so cool, with a mixture of snow, grass, and dead leaves for an outfit. The cold weather didn't bother us nearly as much as the frigid attitude that came from the white man who lived behind us, across the well-maintained alley, as he

Chapter 1: Remembering Moments

entered his back yard with the low-cut, white picket fence.

As he closed the gate, he said, "Hey, you little Niggers, how y'all doing?"

Being naïve, we answered back, "We are doing fine."

Then he yelled another slur as he walked away, "Don't y'all Niggers get that pretty white snow dirty."

"Okay, we won't."

Mama saw us talking to the man and later asked us, "What was that about?"

We said, "He was just saying hi to us Niggers, and don't get the snow dirty."

Mama had a stern look on her face as she processed the information, then she took a pause and asked us, "Do you love yourself?"

We solemnly said, "Yes."

Mama replied, "You are two good-looking boys and you are Negros. However, sometimes jealous or wicked people will call us out of our name to make us unhappy or test our weakness for violence." She told us to defend ourselves by not letting evil words get in the way of what we stood for. If we loved ourselves fully, we should focus on the good that was around us, and everything would be all right. Mama wanted us to speak up about the incident in Sunday School, which we did. She always encouraged us to be real and to know ourselves, especially while living in this big world with so many people and opinions. The "Be Real" habit she taught us encouraged me to live my authentic life from the time I woke up and to always be true to myself.

> *"You are no longer innocent, you are condemned to awareness."*
>
> ~ Michael Eric Dyson

I Grew Responsible

As we got older we found a lot of ways to pass time, like playing sports, hanging out with our siblings, and making new friends in our neighborhood. We had street races in the middle of Ohio Street, played double dare, jumped off the garages, or got pushed off by my brother Sandy if we didn't jump. Sandy was the wild one, a karate nut that we all loved and enjoyed, because he was our protector. It did not take long to connect with our Ohio Street family as we formed a block club, and to this day, we maintain long-lasting friendships with the people who lived on that street. As children, we also enjoyed playing on the same neighborhood baseball team, or being on the same community track team, the Detroit Striders. My sister Charlette and a band of girls ran like gazelles, and they made it to the National Track and Field Youth Games. My brothers and I, who had paper routes or jobs, got tired of listening to her stories and seeing the trophies, medals, and ribbons that my sister won at each of her track events. It did not take long for our jealousy to come out, thinking we couldn't let her be the lone star athlete in the family. We had a plan to get on that team, and Sandy did despite his bow-legged stance. But because I was an asthmatic I had to wait and build up my lungs to be healthy enough to run.

I spent a lot of time in the Children's Hospital's emergency room for asthma attacks as a young child, but I didn't think my asthma was a big deal. Mama and my dad thought my health would be a challenge because of the many episodes that I had with asthma, even when I was not running. But luckily, during one of my follow-up appointments, a Korean doctor told me that one of my problems was that I was not active enough. He gave me the confidence to give the track and field a try. He said when I felt like wheezing, coughing, or had tightness in the chest, to just slow down, take a break, drink lots of water, and exercise my lungs by breathing in through the nose, then out through the mouth. With this new confidence, I worked hard and made the Detroit Striders Track Team, which helped me forge deep connections as we traveled across the country to compete. I learned invaluable information about track and field, as well as life, from our white track coach Marvin Fraser. He was completely devoted to the cause of our team and spent countless days and weekends coaching and teaching many urban black children.

My brothers and I soon found out that making the track team was no excuse for not working a job, as well. Our dad, who was an army veteran, didn't sleep a lot, but got up early in the morning to go to work. He strongly expressed how men in a household needed to get up early, work, and support their families. So, being under my own pressure for staying involved with my paper route and track practice, I had to develop habits to wake up early, be focused in school, and have enough energy to practice in the afternoons. It was still worth the effort because I had the opportunities to experience the choices of going to school, having a job, and being involved with social activities. Yet, I still had to be responsible enough to take care of my paper route by getting a sub when I went to my track meets.

As we grew older and tried to keep up with our friends from the neighborhood and the track team, I started to realize the difference in our financial situations. I could not understand why we did not have at least some of the material things that our family and friends had, like a car to get around in. Although, my dad tried to support us all, I wasn't sure he was capable. I always could hear, or smell, the struggles that came with the alcohol on his breath when he came in from working overtime, with that look of defeat over having a household of nine to support. I felt that we would probably be in a financial trap forever unless someone else stepped up and helped a little more; and that someone else was me.

As crazy as it sounded to my brother Calvin, because I already had a paper route and ran on the track team, I chose to take on a second job, working as a bagger at the A & P grocery store during some evenings and on the weekends. I wasn't paid as a bagger; the A & P security guard, John Williams allowed a few willing boys who wanted to work, to hang around in the front by the checkout lanes, where we positioned ourselves to take the customers' groceries to their cars for possible tips. John Williams went to the same church that I attended, but that didn't mean that he gave out any favors, because he didn't. He ran a tight ship, but he did teach us a few things about proper appearances and how to greet people.

Chapter 1: Remembering Moments

If you wanted to work on the big tip day, which was Saturday, you had to be in line early enough to get picked, because only so many could work. I made a lot of tips on Saturdays, and I had to learn how to maximize my tips by getting up even earlier, so I could beat out the other boys. My willingness to work hard as a bagger for free garnered the notice of the store manager and helped me earn a part-time job in the produce department. Not long after that, however, new management came in with brand-new policies and changes that eliminated my position and the opportunity to make extra money. Mama was my biggest cheerleader for taking on responsibility, and she hated when my dad asked me for money to pay bills. Although I didn't mind helping the family, Mama always told me to put a little money to the side, and no matter what, to save it and do something for myself. I followed her wise advice, and once I started putting a little away, I became more responsible to save my money for the things that I really wanted, and the freedom to buy them. This saving plan also helped me to develop the "Know Money" habit and become more responsible with saving and controlling my spending.

A few months later, Mama told me about a lady named Mildred Frye who, with her husband Albert, owned the A & M Community Market just down the street from the A & P grocery store. I was fortunate to be able to work there, doing odd jobs, while carefully watching and learning the ins-and-outs of owning a business. As my interest in learning grew, I became one of the owner's favorite employees, which did not go over well with some of his children, who also worked there. But, I did not allow them to disturb my plans for gaining as much knowledge as I needed, and I began to consider owning my own business someday. This job gave me the flexibility that I needed with my morning paper route, school, and sports, because I was able to work there after school and still help with family expenses.

When I was not working or at home with my brothers, we learned to turn our misfortunates into fun, by setting examples for our younger siblings. Christmas, in our household, was still a special time despite the fact that we didn't have much money to buy gifts. However, we still had fun sharing gifts with each other. Each year, we took one of our favorite toys or items and wrapped it in comics paper, to give to another sibling. Boy, do I remember the looks of excitement when we received and opened the gifts. One year, Calvin gave me a transistor radio that was in fair condition with a missing knob, but it was like gold to me. We were truly blessed growing up, despite the hardships we experienced.

As the economy shifted, it became harder for the A & M Community Market to keep many employees; therefore, I ended up getting fewer and fewer hours to work. I had to rely on my paper route for more support. I started working to increase my customer base with more door-to-door sales calls, so I would be eligible to be in the paperboy contest. I continued to do my best with my customers by winning just about every newspaper boy contest for sales, and the goodwill promotions that came my way. I became so consistent with winning prizes like radios, watches, baseball cards, or a basketball for new subscriptions and being a thoughtful paperboy, I hid the prizes around the house and later gave them away for birthday or holiday gifts.

Chapter 1: Remembering Moments

Mr. Frye at the A & M market told me, that it was always important to be polite and talk to your customers with a smile. I once watched him make a suggestive sale before he cashed out, and that customer ended up buying exactly what he suggested. I realized that good customer service was an excellent habit, so I followed Mr. Frye's example. I made suggestions to my newspaper customers to change their newspaper subscriptions from a weekend paper to the daily news. I smiled politely when I had to collect from those customers who owed me money, and they always told me to come back. I got to know my customers personally, and the neighborhood kids who lived on my route gave me the nickname "Collect," because they said I didn't mind bugging anyone who owed me money. I could sometimes hear them yelling into the house "Mama, Collect is here;" but my service and persistence all paid off.

Because of my winnings I was known to several of the route managers, and I was later asked by one of them to be his morning assistant. I worked with him to distribute the newspaper bundles to the paperboys' homes who lived far away, and I had to get up even earlier since I still had my own paper route. I thought getting up early was no big deal, since I felt like the boss and I had to be at the distribution office early enough to open it for other newspaper boys, who picked up their papers there. It took quite some time for me to adjust to getting up so early, but it got easier since the extra money was a great incentive. I was so boastful about my job that I often teased my own brothers about their laziness, as they arrived to pick up their papers at the office, looking sleepy and unexcited.

However, I found out that I was a little shy around some people. I remember one uncomfortable moment, in my science class, as I sat on a tall stool at the lab table, running off at the mouth with my friends. Suddenly, I heard a call from my counselor, Mrs. Hartwell on the intercom. She asked my teacher, Ms. Reynolds if Michael Wynn is in class that day. Ms. Reynolds said, "Yes."

Mrs. Hartwell replied, "Tell him not to go anywhere and I will be there in a moment." I got very nervous about what she might want.

When she got to our class she announced, "I was reading the newspaper this morning, and I saw an article and a picture about your classmate Michael Wynn." She passed out one of the articles to the class, as she stood there reading the other one.

> *Michael Wynn is a 14-year old newspaper carrier whose hobbies include coin collecting, bowling, swimming, and model building. Since he acquired his route 2 ½ years ago, he won several trips to Cedar Point amusement park and a district award for his all-round performance as a carrier salesman. The trips and awards are in addition to the radio, watch, tape recorder, and baseball glove he earned by signing up new subscribers. Michael, an eighth grader at Detroit Noble Junior High maintains a B average in school and is a member of the Striders Track Team and the school's library staff. While attending Wayne State University's*

Chapter 1: Remembering Moments

recreation program last summer, he also earned a weight-lifting award. Recently he was nominated one of the Michigan Press Association's Outstanding Newspaper Boys. Besides creating a substantial bank account with the profits from his newspaper route, Michael buys many of his own clothes and helps his parents financially. After completing his education, he hopes to go into business for himself.

As she finished I wanted to sink into the floor, thinking, "Man, she just put all my business out there." It wasn't like Mrs. Hartwell had the only newspaper in town, but I bet none of my classmates would have known had she not shared the article. I was pleased though, that this girl in my class, who I liked, started smiling at me more.

After Mrs. Hartwell read that article to the class, I became the number-one target for the class bullies to get cash. Everyone has fears and I believe it is a natural part of being human, but there are times when fear may keep us from dealing with reality. I cannot believe I gave up my hard-earned money to those boys, yet I felt my options were to give them the money, allow them to beat me up, or let Sandy find out and embarrass me by standing up to the bullies.

The bullying finally came to an end because I was determined to change how I looked physically, so I would not be taken for granted. Over the summer, I got back into my weight-lifting training, admiring and copying body builders like Robby Robinson and Arnold Schwarzenegger. When I got to Mackenzie High School that fall, I was so buff, I was called a 'muscle-bound fool.'

A few months later, I ran into one of the boys that used to bully me in middle school. When he saw me, he did a double-take and said, "Damn! How did you get so damn swollen?"

I replied, "Just doing my thing, staying fit. So, what's up with you?" I stared him down with a slight look of intimidation just to let him know, this was the new Michael.

Suddenly, I felt like I created a new connection with my physical workout program, and the results gave me an attitude boost and more confidence. While in high school, my work ethic remained the same as in middle school. I wanted to make extra money to help my family, enjoy buying my own things, and play sports, so during the summer, a couple of my neighbors and I were lucky to get jobs at McDonald's. It was nice working with my friends and making money while we were still in school. But I had to identify my purpose, passion, and accountability to create my driving desire for a "Target Success" habit, to achieve my goals and objectives with energy.

> *"Good judgement comes from experience, and experience usually comes from bad judgement."*
>
> ~ Anonymous

My Decision Came with Good Judgement

While on the high school track and football teams, I continued to work at McDonald's. After about eighteen months there, I earned the position of Shift Manager. While maintaining about a "B-minus" or "C" average and playing sports, I was tired most days, but I had to keep going because I felt responsible to continue supporting my family financially. We were finally able to afford our first car, a 1970 Ford station wagon with redwood trim that we bought from Mama Hushie's ex-husband. Sandy, the first sibling to get his license, got to drive us around, and sometimes he got to keep the car at school. Because of my busy schedule, I had to work out a system that allowed me to do my homework before going to track or football practice, then get the work on time after practice. With the help from Sandy and the car, I was able to stay above water.

But, for some strange reason, I always felt energized and capable of taking on a lot of things with little sleep. I was somewhat of an outcast socially and not very popular at school. I heard about most of the school social functions after the fact, because I was working or catching up on my homework. But, when it came to the football players and other athletes, they hung out on the second floor of the school, leaning against the lockers between classes. It became a daily gathering for many of them to stand around, talking junk until told to go to class. I was there too, showing off my new clothes, and trying to build popularity among those who were willing to listen.

I hate to admit it, but during this time, the seriousness of my education was only to keep the grades I needed to play sports, because I wasn't thinking about the importance of continuing my education. The only thing on my mind was earning enough money so I could own and run a business with the knowledge I'd gained through working. I didn't think I needed a college education to run a business, because I already learned what business was about from having a paper route and working at the A & M Community Market or McDonalds. Through my high school experiences, I felt like my level of knowledge was above average because I didn't really feel challenged in school, and I could always find a way to get caught up with my homework with no real struggle, if I fell behind.

My brothers Sandy and Calvin, who both graduated in 1975, had their own focuses. Sandy went to work for the Kroger Dairy in Livonia just outside of Detroit, where my cousin William got him a job. He made plenty of money working there, with a lot of overtime. Calvin joined the Navy and went off to Boot Camp in Great Lakes, Illinois, so I just knew I could create my own business without college.

During my senior year, when it came time for me to be focused and prepared for my future, I still had to ask myself, "Why college?" However, sometimes when I got a chance to hang out after school without having to rush to work, I got to see some of my fellow athletes in the gym working out and hanging outside of the back door. I heard a few of the fellows, who also played dual sports, talk about their next step: playing on the college level. They had choices about different college offers they received from being recruited. These conversations piqued my interest, because many of them also talked about the opportunities that they would have in college, regardless of playing sports.

I got to really see and know my coaches as educators instead of sport coaches who were there just to seek championships. I learned a lot from my coaches, like Coach Stan Mullins, who was the Athletic Director and Track Coach at the time. He could always be found after class in the gym, working out with weights before and after track practice with a group of guys, including me. He reminded me of Jack LaLanne, the lifelong fitness guru, nutrition expert, and motivational speaker who was still in top shape when he died at the age of 96. Coach Mullins could put together a team with more spirit than ability yet, teach them to win.

Coach Robert Dozier was my football coach and a highly successful educator who expected and demanded 110% in effort to achieve results. He taught us that practice and repetition created mastery in the game. This lesson gave me an understanding that practice came with habits. Coach Dozier coached many great football players who went to the NFL, including Pepper Johnson, Gilbert Brown, and Jerome Bettis. It was such an honor to have a leader who coached the game on and off the field. I was fortunate that he gave me the guidance to look at college, to advance my sports and career, and to have a profession to fall back on in case I did not play sports professionally. Even if my decision changed about how college fit with my business plans, at least I gave it a chance. Coach Dozier invited college recruiters to come and check out talent during football games, track meets, and other sports, or he provided them with film to highlight the skills of various players.

Before one of my track meets, Coach Dozier informed me that a football recruiter from Indiana State University would be there. After the track meet, I met with the recruiter and Coach Dozier as they explained to me the opportunities of going to college with the skills that I had. After hearing what they had to say, I gave the idea some thought, and it did not take long to convince me that I needed to go to college.

I was offered not a scholarship, but a strong opportunity to earn one later if I came in as a walk-on athlete. Not knowing where the money would come from for the application and testing fees for my college search, I was convinced that I would have to get it on my own. With a family of nine, there was not much money lying around to help with college, but Mama encouraged me to do what I needed to do to be the first one in my family to go to college, which was a great honor.

Knowing that I needed extra money, I worked every chance I got, toiling extra hours, and sometimes entire weekends, while still playing sports. I also attended to my school work so that I maintained a least a 2.5 GPA to get into college. These pressures didn't make me better at what I was doing; they just made me more responsible.

I never thought about how much more I could learn about running a business until I took a business class and joined the school business social club. The classwork and interaction with like-minded students were worth the admission cost, although it took away some of the hours I could work at McDonalds. Yet, the class and club gave me more direction concerning a major and minor for my college journey.

I realized that I really needed to look at making time for change. There are moments in life when we know we need to make a drastic shift. We must stand up to those moments that, while sometimes scary, will lead to a change that will allow us to grow, evolve, and become who we are meant to be.

At graduation, I was amazed that I completed all my academic requirements and was finally ready to be on that stage in front of the crowd filled with family and friends. I gladly accepted my hard-earned diploma, along with 287 other graduates in June of 1976.

But for me to make more of my joy, peace, abundance, and success when I started my college journey, I knew I would have to work hard and develop a Just Win habit to succeed.

"Why not go out on a limb? Isn't that where the fruit is?"

~Frank Scully

The Choices We Have

Go Strong or Go Home

Over the summer, I still received college offers from small schools in Kansas and one in Minnesota, but my mind was made up to go to Indiana State University. In late August 1976, I was ready to go head off to college, sporting an afro, thick sideburns, and my blue-jean vest. I loaded my dad's 1973 white Chevy Impala with my black trunk and other essentials, as I processed that I was on my way to college. My boy Willie, who played on the same football team at Mackenzie High also got a walk-on invitation for the Indiana State football team. Willie became my best friend; he was my college roommate and later the best man in my wedding. Mama and Dad were honored to drive us to Terre Haute, Indiana, about six hours away from home, to drop us off at school. This journey was my first realization that I better go strong with my studies or be prepared to go home if I didn't take advantage of the opportunities that came with attending college.

We got to Indiana State that evening just before dusk. We said our goodbyes to Mama and Dad, then after a moment to check out our room in Hines Hall, we half-unpacked. Quickly, we headed to check out some of the girls' dorms, like Mills Hall, where we saw some of the prettiest women hanging out with guys who looked like they might have a little game, but they had nothing on us. We wanted to be seen as some good-looking dudes with a little edge, but smooth and so cool, with that Detroit flavor. That episode was our first taste of college life, before the grind of the gridiron and hitting the books began. We made new friends from all over the Mid-West. We did hear about another guy at Indiana State from Detroit, but we weren't in a hurry to meet him, because we wanted to be known as the dudes from Detroit. Our fellow Indiana State football players referred to me as "Rabbit," because they said I ran like a rabbit, and they called Willie "Chilly Willy," because he was so laid back.

I had a girlfriend named Angie, back home in Detroit, who had one more year in high school to go. However, I was learning about freedom for the first time, so when I got to Indiana State, I may have been a little flirtatious with other girls as I developed many friendships with people.

So, there was college life: freedom, responsibility, accountability, hard work, and commitment... or the lack thereof. During the first few months I experienced the hard football practices that came before and after classes, going to away games, and fulfilling some rookie duties like getting the veterans towels, water, or Gatorade. I was involved with Alpha Phi Alpha, a pre-interest group to see how life would be in a fraternity, though I never joined one. I hung out at the Indiana State basketball

Chapter 2: The Choices We Have

games because it was so important to be seen at a game where Larry Bird, who later became an NBA superstar, displayed his amazing antics. And we had to hang out at the library at night with the study group, as we contemplated how hard we should actually study. In fact, I was convinced of the rumors that college professors just loved football players on campus, so I didn't have to study that long. Well, that report was not true, because I found out quickly that my buffed body, charming spirit, and convincing smile didn't help me get on my instructors' good side, especially when it came to late course work, incomplete assignments, and a plea for a tutor late at night when the work was due.

This experience was my first chance at freedom, and I already wasted valuable time. My realization that good habits could be useful caused me to pause, because I felt like I was setting the standard for bad habits. I stayed up late, ignored any preparation for pop quizzes, and didn't start my day with the Just Win habit that I had developed in my youth. I remembered what someone once told me about judgement; "Good judgement comes from experience, and experience usually comes from bad judgement." In college, bad judgement became normal for me. I thought I could pull off success like I had in high school, by not being totally prepared. I tried to catch up by glancing at my materials in the morning, looking at the pages that the majority of the class had studied, then B.S. my way through a presentation or quiz. I thought that if I could pull off some decent grades like I did in high school, while working a job, playing sports, and studying when I got a chance, then I would be okay.

However, my scheme did not go as planned, and I did not do so well with my mid-term grades. I was not happy with myself after the first few months of college, and as my first visit home neared, I was concerned it was probably not going to be a good one. I hoped to keep my little personal disaster to myself, because I had a plan to catch up and improve before the final grade was set.

But, when I called home for Thanksgiving, my sisters, who were my main cheerleaders for my college journey, did not take long to let me know that Mama had received a copy of my grades and she was not happy. I had to quickly adjust my work ethic before it was too late to embark on my business goals for the future. As a business administration major, I had to be realistic in adjusting my study habits first, then in practicing and conditioning for football, since I hoped to earn a scholarship the following year. This new focus meant I had to deal with the pain of having a limited social life.

We still found a way to have fun; Thursday night gatherings on the third floor of Hines Hall where I stayed, included card games, food, and friends to get some relief from the week. If it was during the season; the walk-on football players, most of us on the second string, played on Thursday. If it was a home game, we showed up on the third floor to brag about our win or loss. But most importantly we cheered on the varsity

Chapter 2: The Choices We Have

football team, hoping to be the next one to rise in the ranks. All these activities meant I still did not get much studying done during the week.

After the season, I looked forward to hearing from the football team's offensive coordinator, on his decision concerning my future at Indiana State. I had gained some momentum in my studies and tried hard to catch up and improve my sorry GPA of 2.01. I was more serious with my attitude and was making the necessary adjustments on responsibility. Some of the upper-class football players were impressed with my low-style running as a fullback, and they gave me confidence in my hopes for playing the following season.

But as my luck would have it, the day before my Economics and Introduction to Literature finals, I was attacked by a bat in my dorm. That's right; a bat was flying around on the second floor in our dorm, entertaining many of the male students. As I heard all the yelling, I walked into the hallway, and the bat flew frantically into me, catching hold of my shirt collar. I took off running, swinging my arms like a mad man. While trying to free myself from this flying varmint, I swung and hit the glass case for the fire extinguisher equipment, catching my left hand, and ripping my finger on the steel rim. I saw my middle finger split wide open and there was blood everywhere. I passed out, just as I thought I heard someone say, "The bat bit him!" When I woke up, I was in the University infirmary where I saw

Willie standing by my bedside. I was later told that someone sprayed the fire extinguisher to subdue the bat, then took it to the infirmary for testing. Luckily, the lab test showed the bat did not have rabies, but I had to have many stitches that were necessary to fix my finger and hand.

Because of this incident, I missed my finals and I did not have time to make them up before meeting with the football team offensive coordinator. I met with him before spring break in his office. He praised my improvement on the field, but he did not waste any time telling me that he was disappointed with my grades. He told me at that point, he wouldn't ask me to return to play varsity football nor would I gain any assistance from the football program.

As he reached to shake my hand to wish me good luck, for few seconds, I remembered a similar feeling from once before, when my community's track coach, Marv Fraser asked the team to come to a cross-country meet with extra clothes packed. If we ran a qualifying time in the meet held at Palmer Park in Detroit, our reward was a trip to a National Cross-Country event in New York. But, I didn't make a qualifying time. My bag was packed and already loaded on the red Detroit Striders van, and I was so embarrassed when I had to walk past my teammates to remove my stuff from the van. Mama and Dad waited to take me home, while I watched the other team members drive off in the red van.

Chapter 2: The Choices We Have

The meeting with the offensive coordinator was yet another bad day, hearing the toughness in the voice of a Coach who praised me, then made a decision that didn't include me or my future. In that moment, I learned that the Target Success habit involved having an action plan to stay organized and to create a time management system with controls that allowed me to be prepared at all times.

In football and in college, I learned once and for all that:

I had to GO STRONG and be ready to make the necessary sacrifices,

Or, GO HOME in misery, as a failure.

I didn't go strong, so I had to go home, because I knew there was no way my family or I could afford the bills that came with an out-of-state college dream. In May 1977, at the end of my first year of college, I basically disappeared without truthfully telling many of my close football friends, that I would not be returning. Instead, I lied and told them I couldn't wait to return for the next season, a stronger and quicker full-back. Willie was one of the few who knew I was not returning. Instead, I got a head-start on packing my stuff and my memories of Indiana State University. Willie and I took the bus, and it was a long, quiet ride home.

"The secret of success is learning how to use pain and pleasure instead of having pain and pleasure use you. If you do that, you're in control of your life. If you don't, life controls you."

~Tony Robbins

Momentum Is What I Need

Once I was back home, it was hard to return to my old bedroom and answer the many questions from my younger brothers and sisters. They wanted to know how college was, did I have another girlfriend, did I run a touchdown, and oh, how come I wasn't going back? I thought, "Man, how did that cat get let out of the bag so quickly?" But, I forgot that my grade report was sent home to Mama and had been the topic of the family discussion. They had high expectations for me, probably higher than the ones I had for myself.

I took a cowardly approach and did not talk to anyone for a while, just so I could adjust to being home without a job and unsure about my future. After a couple of days, I had to begin answering some of my telephone calls; one of them was from my girlfriend Angie. She invited me

Chapter 2: The Choices We Have

over to her house because she was having a family gathering. I knew her family was really into education and achievement since her mother, aunts, and uncle were teachers, and she had an uncle, who was a Harvard Law School graduate that specialized in educational law, so I knew I had to be ready for some questions. There would be a lot of people at her house who would be happy to see me, but I decided, if anyone asked about my college experience, I would stick to saying, "It was a true experience."

As I walked up her sidewalk, I saw members of Angie's family everywhere I turned. Just as I got in striking distance, the questions started flying from every corner, from people who were excited to see and hear from me. "How was your first year in college?" "How were your classes, and how many did you take?" "Did you play football on offense or defense?" "Did you ever see Larry Bird play basketball?" And then there was that one question, I hoped no one would ask, but her cousin Brian asked it, "With you being so fast, did you make the starting football team?" With a blank look on my face, and a slight shrug of my shoulders, I said, "I hope so." With so many questions being thrown my way, I felt like I was dying inside and couldn't wait to get away. I just wanted some time to think about my next move.

In the weeks to come, I knew I would have to build up some momentum to find a job, save some money, and get back into college, wherever that might be. After a few days, I got used to being home, but I realized that life had changed while I was at college. My dad was not seen at home as much, and my siblings filled me in on some of the problems that Mama and my dad had because of his drinking and the family financial problems. Not to make any excuses for him, but I could understand the difficulties that came with carrying the load of providing for a family of our size. However, I could not go along with him yelling at Mama, so after a couple of altercations that I had with him, some that became physical, I thought it would be best for me to move out and live upstairs at Mama Hushie's house.

My first move was to get into a community college during the summer to build my grades and find some work. I did not yet have a job, but I had some savings left, though that was going fast. Mama Hushie agreed not to charge me rent until I got a job. After some quick maneuvering with student loans, I started attending Wayne County Community College (WCCC), to build my grades up and stay true to my dream of running my own business. For a while, I held out from going back to work at McDonalds, because I knew I would see some of the people who were expecting me to succeed in college. However, it was the only job available with the flexibility I needed while taking classes at WCCC. It helped that I was able to go back and work for the owner Tom Watkins, a former NFL football player for the Cleveland Browns, Pittsburgh Steelers, and the Detroit

Lions. McDonalds was like a family and if you left on good terms, you were always welcomed back.

Just a few months later, I had to face the music, since everyone realized I was not going back to Indiana State in August. Willie, who had a better chance of making the team than I did, decided not to go back to Indiana State, but instead he joined the Detroit Police Department. He wanted me to join as well, but that was just not in my plans. I looked forward to going back to school. As Angie got ready to start at Michigan State University (MSU), I found many excuses not to be around her, because I was embarrassed that I started college a year before her yet found my way back home quickly. This situation gave me more of a drive to get my life together. I had so much ambition, and I knew I would deliver on my promise to Mama to graduate from college, especially, since my younger siblings also looked up to me and questioned my decisions. My brother Fred, who was a year younger than me and still in high school, was the real deal when it came to a hustle. He found work when he needed to and was very creative with buying and fixing up cars and working on them. He told me that he was around to look out for Mama, but I needed to get back into school and follow my dreams of having a business, so he could work for me some day.

Once Angie left for college, I tried to stay focused on what it was I had to do to get back into college by getting the most out of my classes at WCCC. I continued going to work every day at McDonald's and sometimes had to wait on people I knew. Most of them were either getting ready to leave for college or had some plans to land an exciting job that paid a lot more than what I made. I looked the part of a Shift Manager with some authority, wearing a white shirt, black tie, and a paper McDonald's hat that said Manager. Yet, when I saw these people while I was working in the lobby, either cleaning it up myself or, working on the next Ronald McDonald promotion, I felt down on myself. I'm not implying that working at a McDonalds did not have a good future, because some employees went on to become regional managers or even owners. But at that time, it just wasn't my dream to be a worker bee making peanuts, while helping build someone else's dream to be rich. My desire was to find the momentum and money to get back into the game to Just Win, and it wouldn't be at McDonalds.

Chapter 2: The Choices We Have

"The only way for a fighter to get in shape is to fight his way back."

~Sugar Ray Leonard

Had to Rethink my Opportunities

One of the things Mama taught me was to Be Real and to learn how to make peace with yourself and others; to forgive and go forward. In order for me to go forward, I had to sit down with my dad and talk about the family situation. One of the things that worked in my favor, was I continued to visit my family on Ohio street. I was the oldest guy left hanging around the block, so it seemed weird. Sandy had moved out to live on his own while working at the Kroger Dairy and was making some mad money; he even bought himself a new car. Calvin was in the Navy, and Fred was just about to finish high school.

While checking on my family one time, I had a chance to have a conversation with one of our longtime neighbors, Mr. Bartlett. He was a Service Manager at Firestone Tires, and since he knew about my work ethic, he asked me if I was interested in a job. After a few minutes of conversation, I liked what I heard, so told him I would love to work there as the Tire Service Assistant. I was on a mission to make more money, so I was rethinking my opportunities. Since this job paid a lot more than McDonalds and was not too far from WCCC, the decision was a no-brainer. At Firestone, I learned a lot about being flexible to help with other job assignments, especially when I did not have any tires to mount. I helped out the mechanics and did other odd jobs. The flexibility that I learned on this job taught me how to multi-task various projects, and to do a job right the first time.

With a steady flow of money from my 40-hour work week, I was able to pay Mama Hushie a little more in rent and put away a nice portion of money to return to college or to fund my self-made business dream. I had it made during the summer and fall of 1977, because I had a higher-paying job and access to Calvin's slick 1972 red Dodge Roadrunner that he left behind on one of his deployments. Fred and I were assigned to take care of it. I convinced Fred that I really needed the car a lot more than he did, and that I had the finances to take care of the car until Calvin returned home. While I worked at Firestone, I was able to get all the benefits of the garage, from oil changes, minor brake work, and tire rotations, and I was able to get certain employee discounts. My job at Firestone worked out great, until the winter came. It was cold and wet inside and outside, which was bad for my asthma. Sometimes I had to change tires outside, or I had to lie on the ground of the cold, wet garage, which made me sick. I got behind on my classes because I was sick so often, but I was not ready to quit just yet.

During one of our Wynn family Christmas gatherings, however, Sandy came over to me and told me Kroger's

Bakery was hiring. I needed to find out about the job, because I could use more money; it was all about the growth, the quicker the better. I went through the process of applying, and I asked Mr. Bartlett for a reference. That was my way of telling him that I had to quit Firestone to move on to a better-paying job where the work was inside. I explained that the new job would help me reach my goal for getting back into college. Mr. Bartlett said he couldn't blame me for that, so he wished me well and agreed to give me a good reference.

After a few months at Kroger, I was told by the foreman that I was doing a good job, and that I should keep up the good work. It was nothing for me to shine because I was all about making the right impression, but that determination came with challenges.

At lunch time, many of my co-workers hung out in the parking lot eating, drinking, or smoking. However, I wanted to learn all I could from the job so that I could get overtime hours and earn more money for college. I was challenged. I didn't want to seem like some kind of spy because I was seen talking to the management. But, because we worked in a closed union shop, that was exactly what some of my co-workers thought. To fit in, I felt tempted to indulge in some of my friends' lunch plans to drink a little alcohol and smoke some marijuana. But, I kept in mind the opportunities that I could have, so I had to pull out one of my old college excuses, especially after giving up some of those bad habits.

When the "wacky tobaccy" was passed to me at lunch, I played the asthma card saying, "Naw, I'm cool. I can't get with that now, I'll be sick as a dog." But my co-workers never gave up on trying to get me involved. They tried to push a can of beer in my jacket pocket, as I made another excuse about needing to go pay a bill. I wasn't a saint, but I respected my job enough to know I had to be physically ready and alert, just in case some overtime came my way. I was focused on my studies, on working out to hopefully make the MSU football team, and on getting one of the high-paying 3rd shift jobs, so I wasn't willing to jeopardize my health or safety. By this time, I was really focused on my Live Health habits and stayed true to my health-wellness, so that I could still be in shape to play football.

It was just about eighteen months after I left Indiana State, and I was still taking classes at WCCC and looking forward to my return to a college away from home, when I heard about another opportunity. Kroger management was looking for people to join their team, and it was rumored that I was one of them. The management rumor made my decision difficult, because I still wanted to play football at MSU, so I could be with Angie while I went to college. But it wasn't long before I knew the direction that I needed to take.

I was always a little jealous when I went up to East Lansing to visit Angie at MSU, because I got the sense that she had secret admirers. I couldn't be too obvious

Chapter 2: The Choices We Have

that it was a concern to me, because I remembered that when I went away to college, I felt free as a bird. In the fall of 1978, I told Angie I wanted to start at MSU the following spring, since I needed more time to save some money. She was really excited about my decision, so I started the application process and was accepted into MSU. During the Christmas break, Angie and her cousin Sherry, who also went to MSU, approached me with an idea that we all stay together in an apartment. With a plan like that, we could all save some money on living expenses.

With the blessing of her mother, I agreed to the plan. This opportunity was a game changer in making up my mind to go to MSU, and not staying to work for the Kroger management team. I still had some uncertainty, because I thought it might be better to just give up football and stay with Kroger a little longer to make more money before I returned to college. But, I made my decision to go to MSU.

Once I made my decision to go to MSU, it came with a serious commitment. With football on my mind, and my dream of learning more about running a business while in college, I knew I had to focus on both, and this would require some hard work. I was a business administration major at Indiana State, but while taking classes at WCCC, I took accounting classes and did well. So, I decided to major in accounting at MSU. Although I was accepted at MSU as a transfer student, I still had to have a discussion with one of the deans of the Eli Board College of Business to get into the accounting program. The classes were closed out unless there was special consideration. Since I had taken most of my business classes at community college, I pushed to get into the College of Business, because I needed to start right away and did not have any time to waste.

Angie recommended that I talk with her uncle, Lawrence Patrick, who had many connections because of his status as a well-known lawyer from Harvard who also did a lot of community work in Detroit. As it turned out, Lawrence (affectionately called "Buddy") did have the connections that I needed. However, Buddy strongly warned me, as he would do with others seeking advice or connections, that just because he set up the meeting did not mean it would work in my favor, unless I used my skills and talent to convince them I am the one. I told him that I had no choice but to be ready to meet this committee person and be ready to display my best qualities, tools, and wisdom that he knew I had. I thanked him for his encouragement, and I was ready. After the meeting, I was accepted into the accounting program. I was always ready for a change in plans, and this opportunity to use my habits to Target Success made me feel that I was moving forward on the right path.

MSU was on the quarter system instead of semesters like Indiana State. I had to learn about all my required courses and labs, along with the spring football program schedule, because I hoped to join the team as a walk-on, and I needed to be ready. After getting situated in my apartment lifestyle with two women, I had to be up early and ready, with an energetic attitude to be prepared for tomorrow, which meant doing my best each day. Prior to the start of the spring football season, I had a chance to work out at the same gym as some of the football players. I also was able to meet a couple of assistant coaches and the training coordinator, as we discussed how the spring training program worked for the walk-on spring football players. Somehow the conversation turned to my sports background that included baseball, track and field, and football. The coaches saw me as someone who was engaged actively in sports and a person with some endurance. By the end of the month, I was told I was accepted in the program, and that I would run 300-yard dash workouts with some of the starting football players.

I spent a lot of time on campus, trying not to repeat the same mistakes as I made at Indiana State. My days were filled with classes and a work-study program at one of the agriculture labs, because I still had to find a way to finance college. The work-study program gave me some relief with my rising debt. Even with federal loans and my savings, I still struggled financially. However, I was able to stay focused and make the spring practices without worrying about the fast pace of the regular football season. Even with the daily workouts and practice, I still had to stay on top of my class work. I did okay in my accounting classes, but sometimes I had difficulty understanding the foreign-speaking professors or teaching assistants. I had to get a tape recorder and spend a lot of time listening to replays of lessons to get a better understanding of the accounting and statistics formulas. It was hard to stay above water, but I'm glad I knew how to manage my money and press my desire for a winning spirit to keep digging deeper.

Just before the spring game and the selection of which walk-on football players would be allowed to participate, I went in for my required meeting with the athletic office that transfer students had to attend before officially being eligible for a university sport. I thought I had everything in order as I met with a very delightful advisor. He informed me that MSU courses were offered on a quarterly basis. To convert the semester credit hours that I took at Indiana State and WCCC into the system, I had to repeat or take additional courses to become fully eligible for the fall quarter. As optimistic as he sounded, it was not in my plans to repeat classes just to play sports. Although, everything he said made sense, the news just wasn't something I wanted to hear. His recommendation was to give it a try because either way, to graduate I still had to complete that process to gain eligible course work. Although, this news was a big setback, I did not feel like it was the end of the world. I had to reevaluate my opportunities, and in my mind, my priority became the importance of completing college and making my mother happy.

Chapter 2: The Choices We Have

I put spring football behind me, and I went on to take other classes, because either way, I would be able to use them in my journey to complete college. With more free time available, I took the opportunity to find some work, since my savings were getting low, and my work-study program was only a credit to my expenses. One evening, I was walking out of a Quality Dairy store in East Lansing and saw one of my old friends from Detroit who was also going to MSU. During our conversation, he told me about a job at a Firestone Tire Company. I was happy to hear that it was a Firestone, about eight to ten miles away from campus, because it was a company where I had some experience. I walked into the store, chest out, tight hand shake, and a smile on my face, as I explained to the manager that I worked at a Firestone in Detroit and I knew the job of the Tire Assistant, which could save the company the cost of training. The manager was impressed, and I got the job. Being employed again felt good. The routine of going to school and working was a normal event for me. As I adjusted to the area, I noticed that there was a Davenport Business College two blocks from Firestone which might be a better fit for me because of my situation with completing college.

Our apartment near campus was part of a popular apartment complex for student residents. Angie and I took long walks through downtown East Lansing, along Grand River Avenue and through the MSU campus, talking about our future together. As I thought more about our living situation, I fell more in love with Angie.

She was an only child, who didn't really have a lot in common with me, but I liked being around her. Our living situation was becoming harder to deal with, and I longed for some privacy, so I could have my girl to myself. So, I started investigating the possibility of moving out of the apartment after the lease was up. I think the one skill most responsible for the abundance in my life at that time was the ability to enjoy what I had, like a job and a girlfriend who understood me. As I learned how to effectively set and achieve some of my goals, like having a job to support us and being able to stay current in school, I remained positive about owning my own business someday.

About the time we were looking to move in the late spring, there were so many activities going on that we decided to delay moving for a moment. During the basketball season, you couldn't help but be at an MSU basketball game. There was so much hype and excitement around MSU's winning season with Earvin "Magic" Johnson, leading all the way to the 1979 National NCAA Basketball Championship. The wildest thing for me, was that MSU played Indiana State in the championship game. It was Magic Johnson versus Larry Bird, and both had great skills. During the summer after MSU's win, it was hard for us to enjoy the apartment club house and swimming pool because of all the people and celebrations. Once the winter is over, you not only get to see the beauty and greenery around you, but you also find out who lives near you. I always noticed a few

Chapter 2: The Choices We Have

tall guys either walking or driving to the apartments in the back of the complex, but I didn't realize it was Magic Johnson and his teammate who lived there! I finally understood why the pool area was always crowded, especially after the winning season.

After he was drafted to Los Angeles Lakers as the first pick, I thought about Magic Johnson's Just Win story, as a very determined, committed player who obviously had excellent habits with his basketball training. He became one of the youngest players that played several positions for the Los Angeles Lakers. I had always believed, if you followed your dreams, you could achieve anything. After hearing about all the possibilities that Magic Johnson would have with his NBA career, fame, and all-star status, his story became an inspiration to me. For me, making decisions that helped me shape my own destiny put me back in the game to Just Win with the opportunities that I had.

I was convinced even more that I had to move on to a convenient and committed plan to get through college and start my own business. That also meant I had to finally give up my football dreams. It was not hard for me to make the decision to go to Davenport Business College, just down the street from where I worked, because this institution accepted all my transfer credits, and I did not have to repeat any classes. This change was a great option for me, and since we lived in the same metro area as my job and school, I didn't have to worry about moving right away. As the fall term ended, I knew that I worked hard to do well in my classes. Soon, I received the news congratulating me that I earned the honor of being placed on the Dean's List! The Director of Instruction told me that it was extremely important for people to make the most of their opportunities while in college. This small win gave me a big boost to celebrate. I felt great about the work and effort that I had to put forth to get this achievement, but I knew I still had a long way to go.

While Angie was still in school, she supported me in every way I could imagine, with her amazing patience and the motivation that I needed at that time. This encouragement also helped me to visualize the confidence that I needed for my future, which would include her. Therefore, I asked her to marry me and she accepted. We planned a July wedding during the summer of 1980 and made plans to move into MSU's married-student housing on campus.

I got another job at Schaefer Bakery in Lansing. This was a good job for overtime, which helped us to catch up on some bills after our move. While working at Schaefer Bakery, I made many friends there, but it was this one particular guy named Rodrigo Marinez, we had a lot in common like coming from a big family, working out with weights, do-it-yourself advocates, and enjoying the outdoors. He came from a large family with ten children, that he enjoyed being with. He invited me over for some

Chapter 2: The Choices We Have

of his family gatherings to enjoy good times and delicious Mexican cuisine. Rod helped my family out in many ways, and to this day, he remains one of my best friends. Life was going well, with my job to support us while in school, which was nothing new, because I done this balancing act many times before. By Visualizing Faith, Targeting the Success that I wanted, and Thinking about how to Repeat a process to achieve my goals, it became easier to attack situations.

However, living in East Lansing was much different than living in Detroit when it came to rushing or driving faster than I should. The East Lansing Traffic Police were notorious for their speed traps. Before I moved into the University Village on campus, I often drove faster than the speed limit when running late to class or work. Well, that all caught up with me at my last traffic stop because I already had tickets that resulted in 11 points on my driving record. I had to go to the Secretary of State Drivers Improvement Division for a review. I was informed that my license was restricted for the following six months, and that I could only drive to and from work.

This restriction on my driving made scheduling for school, work, and overtime very tough. Meanwhile, Angie became pregnant with our first child. I did the best that I could to stay in compliance with my restricted license requirements, until one night when Angie had some problems sleeping. I didn't know what she needed, so I offered to drive to a convenience store to get her some snacks. What should have been a quick, easy ride back home, turned into a stop by the campus police, because I forgot to turn my lights on as I left the store. As soon as the female police officer asked me for my driver's license, I knew I was in trouble for driving on my restricted license. She wrote me a ticket and told me since I wasn't that far from home, she would follow me home; otherwise she could make me leave my car, and I would have to pay for towing and storage.

It didn't take long to learn the fate of my violation. I was slapped with a one-year driving suspension, which meant no driving whatsoever, or I would go directly to jail. Therefore, while working midnights, I had to purchase a bike and ride it to and from work, half a mile past some corn fields in the dark night. Sometimes I took the slow bus ride from work to school to home, if I was lucky enough to catch it. Either way, my suspended license just added so much chaos to our life. But, we accepted our blessing that I had not been arrested, which could have cost us more money and headaches. Sometimes bad habits, like ignoring a rule, the law, or your own advice, can get you in more trouble than you expect.

Angie graduated from MSU in December 1981, with Michael Jr. on the way, so I had every reason to be happy for my family. The one quality of visualizing faith that I got from Mama was with faith, there is no reason to show your frustrations, because you already accepted a positive outcome. In a year's time, I was back driving

Chapter 2: The Choices We Have

with no restrictions, and I looked forward to rebuilding my driving record for the future. I also finished up my last two terms of college.

During that same time, Rod and I worked out in a lot at different gyms and at his house. I needed these workouts to stay in shape, because it helped me with my focus. The results I got from working out were good, considering I had not worked out for a while and I was pleased to just stay in shape. However, one of the gym owners told me about the Mr. Lansing Body Building contest, and a couple of the guys at the gym dared me to enter. But, it was Rod who convinced me to compete. Although, I had read about body builders when I was in high school, I knew nothing about posing or competing. Some of the people at the gym gave me pointers on how to succeed with the competition. Rod attended the event to support me, and out of 10 finalists, I won third place! Pictures and the results were shown in the Lansing Journal newspaper, and I shared the article with my family, especially my youngest brother Greg, who was very proud of me. Altogether, this contest was another win to boost my confidence. It also showed me the importance my health regimen played in my physical ability to compete, in just a short period of time.

In February 1982, Michael Jr. was born. It is a father's dream to have a son as his first child. As I enjoyed the moment of his birth, I thought about the living legacy that we would provide for him while he grew. This year was amazing for me because I got through all of the remaining business courses as planned, and I graduated from college in June. As proud as I was to be the first in my family to graduate from college, I knew I made Mama and my family even prouder. I had done my best for that moment, but I looked forward to being in an even better place with my career, growth, finances, and many other opportunities to come.

"Mind is a flexible mirror, adjust it, to see a better world."

~Amit Ray

In Search for a Fixed Mindset

The Misfortunes of Work and Business

"The job is yours if you want it," I was told. Working at Schaefer Bakery, for about 30 months provided me with many opportunities. I learned a lot about the distribution operation, management, labor issues, and numerical ordering for distribution. So, it was not a surprise when one of the general managers asked me to have lunch with him. We walked down the street to have lunch and during our conversation, he told me how impressed he was that I studied during my lunch hour in the break room. He also commended me for having a positive attitude when we had to work emergency overtime without a prior notice. As he established that he was interested in me for a supervisory or administrative position, I wondered if I would be chosen for a foreman or distribution position. I thought it would also be nice to work in the front office, since we talked about my education, career, and ambitions to work in an accounting and management-related field. However, he told me he was interested in me for an opportunity as a distribution supervisor, but it was not in the Lansing location. He continued to speak about the Jackson, Michigan operation and all that the area offered. I had a lot to consider before I made a decision.

Chapter 3: The Search for a Fixed Mindset

I held back on my decision for a couple of months, because at the time, we lived in Lansing, and Angie was pursuing a job in the field of journalism. It would be difficult to uproot our family to work a job that was in another city and not in my career path. However, before I could give an answer to the general manager, we all received notice that the Lansing operations of Schaefer Bakery were discontinued. We all lost our jobs and were suddenly out of work. All we had to look forward to was an unemployment check which was about a third of what we had been paid. So, with only a letter and the severance payment calculation given to me, I was sent on my way, to fend for myself or to find another job to support my family.

In times like this, Mama said, "You got to step out on faith and don't look back." So, I received my severance pay and my unemployment benefits with the solace of having some money. I was also relieved that I still had employee benefits for the following 30 days. This job loss meant that I was a stay-at-home dad for a temporary period while I planned my next move. Angie worked a short-term job for the State of Michigan, so we did have some other money coming in.

While I was home without a job, I had a chance to research information about running my own business as suggested by one of my college instructors. When I attended Davenport University in Flint, Michigan. I had the most amazing, and energized accounting instructor, that commanded us to call him by his first name, Dallas. Dallas was a laid-back CPA instructor who also had an accounting business on the side. Sometimes, after class, Dallas offered me a ride to my hotel, so I got some extra time to ask him questions about how to start and run a business. He gave me some direction and some understanding of the information that I would need to start a business under Michigan laws and regulations. His best advice was to stay positive with the process of starting a business, take it in stride, but be able to help someone out, once you reached success in your own business. While riding in his car, I heard a motivational tape of Brian Tracy playing at a low volume, while we were talking. It was clear that he enjoyed listening to motivational information. I asked him if he was also a motivational speaker. He said not really, but he liked listening to motivational speakers like Earl Nightingale, Brian Tracy, Jim Rohn, Les Brown, and Tony Robbins to name a few; and he encouraged me to follow up on them. So, when I lost my job and needed to decide my next move, I started studying some of the same motivational speakers, as well as reading Napoleon Hill's book, *Think and Grow Rich*. The information from these speakers gave me a lot of confidence to have a Just Win attitude as I prepared and graduated from Davenport University in June 1982. After graduation, I had a plan and I was excited about gaining some new employment as well as looking into owning my own business.

Chapter 3: The Search for a Fixed Mindset

It took me longer than I thought to find a full-time job, so while working odd jobs to help with bills, Angie got some good news and was offered a job in Detroit, at a minority radio station, as the personal assistant specialist to the vice president of Public Relations. By her accepting this job offer it meant we had to pack up and move to Detroit. Since we had to make a quick decision and didn't have a place to live for a few months, we stayed with her mother and step-father. When I was young, the one thing my dad drilled in my head was to be a man and provide the support for your family as needed. So, once we moved to Detroit, I really had to think like a man and look for a job that would pay enough to support my family.

During the time I was looking for a job, Angie stayed in contact with some of her friends in Lansing. One of her friends told her about some job openings in accounting with the State of Michigan. I saw job postings in the Michigan Department of Transportation, for finance and accounting positions. There was an opening as an auditor in the Office of Commission Audit. I also remember that my instructor Dallas once worked as an auditor, so that's where I focused my attention.

Most entry-level auditors had experience in accounting or finance before they became an auditor, but that did not stop me from applying. I had a great interview, and after that meeting, I set my intentions and mindset to claim this job as mine, using the Visualize Faith habit. A few days after the interview, the full-time position of auditor was offered to me, and I accepted. I found out quickly that this position was a huge accomplishment for me, since I didn't have work experience as an accountant. So, I had to develop habits with an action plan to be organized and study information on the related Michigan and federal highway funding laws, as quickly as possible.

The main down-side of my new job was that I had to arrange a way to get to and from work in Lansing, where my job was located. Many days, I had to drive from my house in Detroit, to Lansing to get to work, which was about 110 miles one way. But as a highway auditor, I also had to travel to many other places in the State of Michigan. Driving myself to work was very demanding, and I decided to join a vanpool of people who supported one another to get to work.

While dealing with several work assignments that required a lot of travel, I also prepared to make a second attempt to pass the CPA exam. In the Office of Commission Audit, an auditor who passed the exam was in a better place for a promotion, although it was not a requirement for the job. There were a few people in the office that passed, in fact, I had a friend who I helped pass the exam, but I was unable to get a passing score on more than two parts of the five-part exam, even after my third attempt. Later in the year, I made a fourth attempt on the exam, but my results were pretty much the same.

Chapter 3: The Search for a Fixed Mindset

My frustration over not being able to achieve this goal deeply annoyed me, because I felt unable to change my situation. I was always on the road traveling for work, so my energy was zapped. As much as I wanted to pass to gain a big reward, because it would be a highlight when I built my own business, it just did not happen for me. However, I discovered letting go of the bitterness about not passing, freed me to initiate a focus process by learning more about my current job structure and business management, which could help me set up my own business in the future.

At first, I was excited to be a minority auditor for the State of Michigan, but I soon realized that my spirit would be tested, as I dealt with a lot of racial tension. While working in an oversight position, I had to travel to northern counties and cities where minorities were less common, especially those having a position with financial oversight responsibilities. These racial tensions were not a new happening in my life, but they continued to show up when I didn't want them to! I was happy and respectful to people, but I guess I expected too much by wanting the same in return. If I exercised my professionalism during an audit or greeted people with a kind and polite gesture, I expected to receive the same back. But that wasn't always the case in the northern part of Michigan.

Once, I was in the city of Menominee in the Upper Peninsula to do a highway audit along with another co-worker. As we walked down the street on our way into a restaurant, a passing car drove by, filled with young white men who yelled out the window, "Go Home Nigger," just as we were entering the restaurant. Many of the people around the restaurant, who heard the slur, looked at me as if I should take the men's advice. My co-worker who was white, however, felt so embarrassed that he tried to comfort me as if I had not been in a situation like that before.

Another incident really had me on the edge for a while, even though I tried to forget about it. At a work site in West Branch, Michigan, I had an assigned area to work in, and one morning, when I sat down, I looked up to see a black toy gorilla dangling from a noose that was tied from a beam. As I looked around angrily, I saw a couple of people who may have wanted to express some sorrow but didn't. I realized that saying anything at that point would only be the fuel needed to carry on for whoever placed the toy. While in these northern cities, I was forced to make the best out of these situations, but sometimes I had trouble just getting a good meal! I didn't feel comfortable being the only black person in a restaurant, especially when I saw a cook, who just prepared my meal, staring me down as I ate. Sometimes, I only ate fruit and snacks in my hotel room, because the fear of eating in some of those establishments forced me to pass on eating out.

Chapter 3: The Search for a Fixed Mindset

I had been in racially tense situations before, but there came a point when I could only express my anger to myself. I knew holding this anger inside was unhealthy because of the job stress that I already dealt with. Having to deal with some emotional turmoil on top of that stress was detrimental. I had to find a healthy way to honor my angry feelings, so I did my best to release them by going for a run or working out at the fitness center before I got home.

After a few years as an auditor, one of those business opportunities that I was looking forward to came in 1992, when I became a real-estate investor. I started buying bargain houses and turning them into rental-income properties. It was a pleasure to rush home from work, so I could go straight to a house that I was renovating. I dreamed about the income that I could produce and have for my children's college funds.

During one of my audit assignments in Detroit, I was able to spend more time with my section manager Greg, who was also a licensed builder and built his own house. He shared some tips with me and told me about the opportunities for getting my builder's license. I didn't think I would build homes right away, but there were so many aspects of the Detroit real-estate market, like home inspections, construction clean-up, and handyman services that were in high demand.

After a few attempts taking the residential builder's exam and applying my Think Repeat habit to journal my intentions, I passed in 1994. The license allowed me the opportunity to engage a little in the construction field. This new opportunity meant I had to really stay on top of the construction codes, while also learning how to keep up-to-date on those all-so-boring audit standards, which were a necessary requirement for my job as an auditor. Having my own business on the side while working a full-time job became the mental relaxation I needed to deal with my stressful job as an auditor.

On most Friday's when I got back in town from traveling for my job, I looked forward to working on my side business because I really enjoyed being an entrepreneur and having the control to be my own boss. However, running a business on a limited schedule was challenging, because it involved having a good strategic plan, multitasking, and plenty of hard work. To avoid frustrations over not completing a task in a timely manner, I thought I could just ignore sleep and honor my "Just Keep Moving" motto. But, when my many undertakings got out of control, I did not have a problem abandoning something that would cause more drama in my life.

As problems grew with my job as an auditor, which was the main means of support for my family, I had to make a decision on the time I spent with rental property. I got to the point that I no longer wanted the drama that came with the rental properties, so I decided to finally get rid of the last local rental property that I owned. This

Chapter 3: The Search for a Fixed Mindset

conclusion came after I stopped to collect rent one day, and I saw the police and an emergency medical unit parked outside of my rental property. My tenant, a single mother, was married when she and her husband first became my tenants. But during the course of renting there were many problems. As the emergency medical unit carried the husband out on a stretcher because of some type of domestic issue. My concern for his estranged wife and child caused unnecessary drama in my life, which admittedly, I allowed. My behavior towards my tenant was shaped by some of the challenging situations I encountered by growing up poor. I never stopped reacting to experiences that reminded me of that time in my life. I also remembered what Dallas suggested to me, that when I owned my own business, I should help someone along the way.

After spending my valuable time listening to the problems of this tenant and giving her advice, I created a method to identify her spending habits, expenses, and obligations. I developed a reasonable payment plan for her to pay her back-rent, then make timely payments. She claimed her government job was enough for a single person to afford the rental agreement. I acted like her personal financial coach for free, and she failed in every agreement for her to get back on track. After another year went by, and I had made every possible attempt to help her, I decided finally I had to sell this property and her tenancy to any willing buyer or real-estate investor. In a last attempt to help this single mom, I told the buyer that her rent was $240 less per month than I had charged. Although this incident did not have the happy ending that I hoped for, it never stopped me from helping people.

A few months later, I started another side business in retail sales and business services, but it was out of a crowded and junky flea market called the County Fair Flea Market. Although, a clutter-filled establishment, this place had plenty of foot traffic on the weekends, so it was more than worth the $52 booth-rental fee that covered Friday evening through Sunday evening. I sold close-out specialty items and prepared income tax returns as well. I found that I was among many people like me, who had stories to tell and valued their time being in the same atmosphere as other weekend entrepreneurs, who took on a greater financial risk to be in this environment. I also spent quality time with my boys to show them a little about running a business and to remind them about of the wisdom my grandfather, Daddy Bradly used to share with me when he ran his dry ice business: "If you mind your pennies, the dollars will flow." His advice gave me an understanding to Know Money and recognize the importance of developing a living and learning legacy. I believe my boys learned something about running a business, but they did not hang out with me much during tax season, which was the slow time of the year at the flea market. However, I always found time to spend with all my children, with activities that enriched their growth.

Chapter 3: The Search for a Fixed Mindset

This weekend business was convenient for me to make some extra money with my crazy schedule, but it also meant that I was absorbed into the flea-market lifestyle, as I watched and listened to some of the people who had been rooted in the flea-market community for years. Sometimes, while sitting and waiting on my next income tax appointment, I drifted away into thoughts of how nice it was to be around peaceful people like those at the flea market. And then, my thoughts shifted to my State job and the Sunday evening preparation for another week to work up north. The stress from that job could cause me to accelerate and lose control, by just being there. I started having more emotional problems with my State job, and I'm sure these issues compounded inside of me.

As I shook my daydream away and looked at this particular lady in the booth across from me, I noticed that she dressed very stylishly, yet she sold second-hand junk. She had about a ten-year supply of pots, pans, fans, sewing machines, and a lot of other stuff; some of which reminded me of items I had seen in a back room of Mama Hushie's house. But for a brief moment, I thought about how great it would be to feel as free and peaceful as she seemed.

As far as my job as an auditor was going, I continued to ignore the fact that I probably needed to make some deep personal changes, instead of the situational changes that I tried to make. My feelings for getting involved with my business dreams were not a sign to me that I failed; I just believed that if I moved from job to job to find my niche, then everything else would work out.

I finally got the nerve to leave my 13 years of employment with the Michigan Office of Commission Audit to take a job in Detroit at the UAW Local 7 as a financial assistant to the financial officer. I had plenty of experience and the right qualifications for the job, but I also had a lot of responsibility because the elected financial officer for the membership did not have a financial background. It was up to me to know the accounting, finance, income tax and payroll rules, along with understanding labor financial reporting. This job gave me a lot of flexibility and working with the members felt like family. Many of them purchased some of my specialty marketing items, and I also did their income taxes on the side. However, after four and a half years there, I found out that I wanted to focus more on my financial accounting profession, even though I enjoyed working in Detroit and the connections that I made.

Soon, another one of my employment journeys started. Stratford, one of my friends, told me about some job openings with the Michigan Gaming Control Board (MGCB), that included posts as auditors. The positions could also result in becoming the auditor-in-charge for one of the three Detroit casinos that were still in the construction phase. Stratford told me more about the opportunities and knowing him, he also does thorough

Chapter 3: The Search for a Fixed Mindset

research, but I did not hesitate to investigate some other details to consider a career with gaming.

The position was involved with the oversight teams to approve and regulate the opening of the casinos. I applied to this position, and during the interview, a couple of the panel members were interested that I had a financial auditing background and a builder's license. I was hired and was later selected to work on the construction-monitoring team, as well as on the background investigations for the casino openings. As an auditor, I also had responsibilities to determine if the casinos followed the minimum internal-control standards and other rules and regulations of the Revenue Treasury Act. Stratford was also hired as an auditor-in-charge, and we gained many opportunities within these positions for growth because we had to monitor the regulations, operations, and promotions of casino gaming for the first casinos in Detroit.

We had to meet with some of the high-ranking casino officials, managers, and investors from Las Vegas for the casino openings. Occasionally, we experienced attempts of intimidation from these sources because of their desire to get the casino properties open as soon as possible. However, I wasn't going to jeopardize my integrity to bend the rules for someone else. We worked with people from various areas of gaming like the State Police, the Internal Revenue Office, the Secret Service, and other

MGCB members of Licensing and Regulations to keep the casinos in compliance.

After two years of my employment with the gaming board, some of the work politics became an issue for me. Because in my strongest opinion of an assignment that appeared to circumvent a department policy, I was told to work on it with others, so it can be done quickly. Many procedures were ignored. Defending my integrity, I was reluctant to join the team which caused a delay, and I became a victim of harassment for many months after that.

At this time in my life I tried not to deal with the intimidation, because the emotional ties I retained from my job at the State reminded me about people who did not respect my rights as a person. I tried taking a professional approach to these matters, but the situation became intense, and my outbursts were heard in the office and public areas of work. I ended up having to put together a series of actions to defend myself through public hearings and legal actions. I stood strong, knowing that I liked my job and my profession, but I would not allow people to intimidate me anymore. This situation made me realize I had to stand up for myself, no matter what. However, the anxiety was not worth the cost to my health, because one morning, I passed out in my office. While lying in the emergency room, I realized that all the complaints and legal actions spelled the end

Chapter 3: The Search for a Fixed Mindset

of my working days with the Michigan Gaming Control Board.

Unfortunately, I came to the conclusion that I had to quit this job to save me from any future employee issues with losing control when defending myself. I enjoyed working with my friends and having conversations with the patrons looking for a friendly voice, about things other than how to better their odds in the casino. But, as a motivator, I felt obligated to share some of the habits I learned to Know Money, and they were bound to listen to information that they considered helpful.

The final straw that helped me realize, once and for all, that I had to find a new job, was when I brought my bad attitude and erratic behavior, such as the yelling and angry comments to my home. Even my children noticed a negative change in me, and I knew I had to have a time-out from work.

"There are roads out of the secret place within us along which we must all move as we go to touch others." ~Romare Bearden

The Family Ties that Matter Too!

Angie and I moved back to Detroit from Lansing, after a year of my employment with the State of Michigan. In 1984, Angie got another job working for a major non-profit insurance company in Detroit, as a community affairs coordinator. As a young couple with a child we were still learning about working together as a family. I had to get used to Angie as an only child, because I saw that my upbringing in a large family was far different. After a few months, we moved out of her mother's house and rented a house from Angie's aunt on the west side of Detroit. We made some adjustments and sacrifices, but there were still financial strains and struggles of not having enough.

We had to brace ourselves against a shift from being patient with each other, to not working together as a team; however, we kept on trying. During the same year, Angie's mother Lynette, who was a wonderful, down-to-earth person, unexpectedly became ill and passed away.

Chapter 3: The Search for a Fixed Mindset

This period was a very difficult time for Angie, and it took a while for her to get over her mother's death because she was the only child and they were very close. About a year later, my second son Patrick was born. Then, since both of us were employed, we were fortunate to buy our first home in Detroit. Home ownership was much easier because we agreed to work with a budget and control our spending.

While I was working for the State of Michigan, traveling during the week, then dealing with tending to my rental property on the weekends, Angie bore the full brunt of getting the children to daycare, school and activities, and it became stressful in the household. There was a lot of pressure on Angie because of the sacrifices and challenges she had to make without any consideration of me being there to help since I traveled so often. The challenges became even greater and more intense, so I found it easier to avoid the conflicts by staying away from home to work on my rental properties. Angie and I did not always share the same vision about having rental property for extra income, so it was easier to avoid what I knew would cause an aggressive conversation that would turn into an argument.

The family ties were disconnected even more, because many times when I got home from work, I headed straight to my home office in the basement with no windows and very little ventilation. I sheltered myself away from the family, so I could claim my time to myself by using it as an excuse to work on my business. This defense was just an excuse to escape because I was unable to control my anger that lingered from my job, and I felt that solitude was the best place to be. Maybe I was selfish, ignoring the fact that Angie was the one who had to stay home to see to the children, but my behavior put a strain on our relationship. Basically, our routine was like a machine that lacked oil and had a few knocks, but we still tried to find something to make us happy.

A few years later our third child Lynette, who we named after her grandmother, was born. The wonderful cry of my newborn baby gave me the motivation to work better at our relationship. Although, we played the part of a happy couple, the love that we had for each other was threatened. We just stopped caring for each other like we used to, and there were little irritations, like who was responsible for certain duties, that became a challenge. However, we continued to deal with the ups and downs, like many couples did, by just putting the problems behind us, in the hope that our relationship would improve.

We did make some efforts to celebrate each other's achievements, like when Angie wrote her first novel, *Every-Thing She Wants*, and the book was a bestseller, published on a mass market. Because of her success, I was willing to help boost our relationship by supporting her in every way. We promoted her book around the country at book stores, coffee shops, family gatherings, and even at our Mackenzie High School reunion picnics. She made good on her skills and accomplishments, and I was proud of her. Though the book tours proved we could enjoy working together, I still dealt with so much discontent that came from my job, that it had a big impact on my family and me.

My anger and frustration of dealing with my jobs always got in the way of my happiness. So, when I got home, it seemed I was looking for a problem instead of offering a pleasant greeting to my family. Angie and I only communicated on a surface level about the kids or work, rather than truly connecting. Even when nothing was going on with us, I continued to be frustrated over little things, and none of this was good for my relationship with my family. I reacted to some of the most ridiculous things, so I tried to find a way to stay away from home until I got my act together. Even if I did nothing but acknowledge what I was feeling, I believed my attitude would alter the way I reacted to different circumstances.

"It's not the load that breaks you down, it's the way you carry it."

~Lena Horne

The Thoughts of Going Crazy

One particular morning in 1995, while I was still working for the Office of Commission Audit, I awoke from a restless night, which was normal for me. However, I was so fatigued, my body felt weak. My internal medicine doctor told me previously that my immune system was low, probably related to the amount of stress in my life. When I left the house at 5:45 a.m., and walked outside towards my car, I smelled a fresh scent from a skunk that was so strong, I could almost taste the residue in the air. I already had a headache, probably from taking a large dose of St. John Wort vitamins the previous night, after a recommendation when my doctor talked to me about stress. I wasn't sure what else was bothering me. The odor of the skunk caused my headache to throb even more, and I was not ready to move as quickly for work as I should've been. Maybe I was looking for an excuse not to go to work, but I experienced multiple symptoms of nausea and exhaustion. I felt like I was going to have one of my crying spells that I had sometimes, but I never shared with anyone. Actually, I didn't want to tell anyone

Chapter 3: The Search for a Fixed Mindset

because I felt comfortable to self-diagnose myself and push the sadness down as part of being overwhelmed. So, I just sat in my car, and after a moment, I pulled it into the garage and shut the door to avoid the skunk's scent.

As I sat quietly in my car in the garage, I realized how out of balance and burned out I felt, from traveling all over the state, to being not available for my family. I also wondered and thought about how hard it was for me to sleep. Most of the time, I laid in the bed, staring at the ceiling, but when I got up after a little rest, I just felt angry. I tried hard not to show that frustration to others when I left home to catch the vanpool for work. While I sat in the car, I heard myself mumbling and reciting something back to myself, without knowing if it just came out of my mouth out of control or did I do it on purpose like some kind of affirmation.

I sat there in the car thinking, "Am I even worthy to have the things I want for my family and me?" But for a few seconds, I wondered, "What if I wasn't here?" I never described what I meant by being absent from all of this, because I didn't want to have an excuse. Wiping my watery eyes, I could only realize what nonsense crossed my mind, and that's as far as I got with that idea, because in my mindset I was a strong man capable of dealing with anything. I gazed at a crooked shelf over the garbage cans that I hadn't noticed before, and thought, "Nothing is left up to chance, but is my job worth going to everyday?" It wasn't like I produced enough income to cover the family's living expenses. We had purchased our five-bedroom house a couple years previously and keeping up with my sons' swimming activities and my daughter's dance and piano lessons were expensive. But for that moment, I didn't care about anything because I was sad and angry with myself.

I finally came to a decision to go on sick leave from work to find out what was going on with my anger and crying spells. If I was 'crazy,' I still believed it was due to being overworked, rather than having any mental illness issues. I went to see a psychiatrist only because my primary care physician was really concerned with my lack of sleep, usually less than four hours a night, and my claims of being functional enough to drive to and from Lansing. I went through a trial period with my psychiatrist and a therapist, so I could be properly evaluated. After my consultation, the psychiatrist suggested that I start taking a medication called lithium. I was shocked by her recommendation because I thought lithium was used to treat bipolar disorders. I turned to the doctor to ask her, "Why do I need this? I just have a problem with sleeping. I'm in control of my day with nothing out of the ordinary." The doctor replied, that based on her assessment, I could be suffering from a combination of bipolar disorder and depression, because of the anxiety, and fear, though she did not feel I was suffering from the strongest symptoms of the conditions. After expressing my concerns and speaking on my limited knowledge about this medication, the psychiatrist was able to convince me that lithium had some good benefits and would give me better balance to help me sleep. I started on a three-month trial.

After 15 days of taking the medication, I started feeling the effects on my body. I was wiped out and didn't want to be bothered by anyone because, I felt like a zombie. At times, I wasn't sure if I was awake, asleep, or in panic mode. If I moved too fast, I felt like a panic attack was coming, or if I moved too slow, the world was caving in. It was so easy to slip into a funk with that empty feeling of sadness. Yet, my doctor convinced me to take another three-month trial period because I did not complete my lab work, so it was six months before I could look at another medication. I wasn't sure why the experts said lithium was the better drug for my condition, a condition that I was not even sure that I had, and I was concerned that I was over-medicated. So, after that six-month period, I had a deeper discussion with my doctor about options. I told her I didn't think lithium worked for me, because I felt sadder than before starting the anti-depression drugs. The medication made me so tired I couldn't think straight, so when the doctor asked if I wanted to harm myself, I just drew a blank. She may have misread my silence for a positive answer about harming myself, but for some reason I was not in a hurry to answer. Then, she informed me that her diagnosis was accurate, and I had a depression disorder and bipolar disorder.

As we continued our conversation, the doctor informed me that she wanted me to start taking Depakote with Prozac instead. My thoughts immediately took me to where I didn't want to go. I began to feel like this issue could be more than a sleeping problem and that I might really be mentally ill. For me, difficult situations had arisen from time to time that I either handled right away or ignored, if I thought I could internalize them. After I found out that I also needed to schedule more psychiatric and therapy visits, I aggressively looked for another job in Detroit, closer to home. I sincerely believed that my job and the commute caused my issues, and I continued to deny that there might be a mental illness that existed within me.

"Lose not courage, lose not faith, go forward."

~ Marcus Garvey

But, Habits Don't Lie

Find Change or Decay

While on medical leave from MGCB for about four months, I had a lot of time to think. I changed my behavior but disconnected with my thoughts of having depression and bipolar disorder, since I accepted it as a state of mind. However, my daughter Lynette, who was 14-years old at the time, told me that's not how she saw my condition. She remembered once, I was so irritated, that I planted 30 trees in a day at a nonstop pace to find a release. She and her girlfriends saw me working like some kind of mad man, which she later described as a manic state.

There were other times when I came straight home from work, got in the bed with my three-piece suit and shoes on, and pulled the covers over my head. I laid there in my favorite 'zombie zone,' moping and trying to drift off to sleep, rather than having to deal with my routine prescription of seeing my doctor, therapist, or group session. It was easier to lie there in bed, blocking out every surrounding moment. I remember being so stuck in my desire to escape, that once, Lynette tugged and tugged on me to get up, so I could take her to dance lessons. However, I just laid there under the covers like a drunk, with slobber coming from my mouth, and I was

Chapter 4: But, Habits Don't Lie

embarrassed that my clothes were soiled because I didn't even feel like getting up to go to the bathroom.

Later, Lynette and I reminisced about how I had come a long way, from not dealing with my disorder, to finally taking some action. She saw me around the house when I had feelings of anxiety, or when I made some decisions on the fly that impacted everyone and our family budget. Sometimes I remodeled the kitchen without giving notice, or I changed a room around in the middle of the night when I couldn't sleep. I sometimes turned my frustrations on Angie because I felt that she didn't express her love enough to me, though I did not give her many reasons to express her love when I lashed out with unkind words and actions. Lynette's recollections of those events were far more accurate than mine. But, during this time of adjusting to more positive feelings, I worked on a habit to Visualize Faith and seek peace around me, until I was ready to go back to work.

Through my pain and suffering, I decided to terminate my employment with MGCB, so I could move on; and it was the right decision. Once I resigned, I was blessed to find a job with the Detroit Public Schools (DPS) in the Office of Internal Audit as a senior auditor. While still having some feeling of anxiety because of a new job and my disorder, I did not want to let others know about my private situation since I was beginning to feel good about myself. This job gave me a sense of appreciation because

I worked among people who were dedicated to protecting the funds necessary for student advancement.

At the time of my employment, the Office of Internal Audit was a very active division in the department. There had been a recent takeover of DPS by the State of Michigan under a school reform bill which placed a CEO over the district operations. When I got there, the office was in the middle of taking on new assignments for review. I met a host of good people, and it did not take long for me to learn the job and enjoy working with my new co-workers. After the orientation, I had some positive feelings of hope that could allow me to create excellent outcomes from this job. I also found out quickly how I valued all my friendships and connections that were created in this close office unit of people stationed inside a small, white Victorian house. It was a peaceful place to work.

One of my co-workers Jeff made it easy for me to get personal, without him knowing about my disorder. He had so much insight, that he became a very close friend, part of the circle of friendships for responsive change in my life. There were also unique relationships that enriched my life, like my friends Bernadette and Kandekye from Uganda, who always shared the riches of their birth country with me, like their food, families, and stories that allowed me to think outside of my crazy world. Terri, who worked with me on various assigned projects, and her husband Roy, who worked in the

Chapter 4: But, Habits Don't Lie

general counsel office, reminded me of a model and loving couple that enjoyed working in the same environment. And my co-worker Edyth shared some of her knowledge and skills with me from her previous employment.

All these friendships were rewarding connections. With such rich spirits around me, I felt empowered to get my certification as a fraud examiner, which was something that I had wanted to do for a while. Becoming a fraud examiner was a great opportunity for many reasons; I was a vessel to safeguard the resources of the students in DPS, and a protector against identity theft and fraud for many elderly people. Despite my disorder, in 2003, I was focused enough not only to complete my certification, but I was asked to write a bi-weekly article in the Michigan Citizen newspaper about Financial Focus. This opportunity allowed me to help many others.

What I learned, is that when I developed habits to believe in myself, these habits forced me to try to move forward, which in turn, got me to make progress with the positive changes. Feeling that I could help others gave me the faith, motivation, and energy to move forward, without thinking about the disorder that took me to many dark and unmentionable places. Once I felt positive-more, I feared-less; I was unstoppable.

I worked hard to repair myself, yet I realized that the love Angie and I had for each other as a married couple had low chemistry at best. A couple of times we discussed ending our marriage, so we could at least save our friendship by being true to ourselves. There was one time we had a unique couple's assessment for our marriage, and with that one session, the results came up with the same conclusion that we had. The results indicated that we would be better off divorcing, not because we showed a lack of love, but because it seemed like we had given up trying. I should not have been surprised at the results, knowing the way I reacted to every moment of a potential problem, my outbursts, or any misunderstanding in our household, but I was stunned to think my marriage might be over. I just couldn't give up like that, however, because I had too much pride in taking care of my own children, at least through high school. We were good parents to our children, and it was important for us to see to their needs.

So, I just went back to work, ignoring any suggestion from my psychiatrist and the results of the assessment. After a few months went by, I had to make a medical change to my health plan, so I began to see a different psychiatrist and therapist, who were covered by my new health plan.

My new psychiatrist continued my medical treatment as it was, but he developed a plan based on feedback from my therapist. After meeting my new therapist Melissa, I knew right away that her positive energy would transfer to me. She had a very subdued voice but was excited about helping me. Right away, she cared more about

Chapter 4: But, Habits Don't Lie

where I was in the moment, instead of where I had come from. After asking several questions, she helped me to intentionally get on the right path with my physical and mental health, which included getting in touch with myself. Within three years, I was able to make one of the best transitions in my life, cleansing my body from the anti-depression drugs.

As I worked with Melissa through counseling, she got me to understand how to recognize those habits that worked best for me. Her wisdom reminded me of Mama, as even during difficult circumstances, she helped me to enjoy myself with daily affirmations, reading more from motivational experts, and exercising my body and mind, including yoga, meditation, and physical weight training. Her overall goal was to help me to learn how to set intentions for a positive outcome. She encouraged me to flush out the negative and make room for the positive. She really got me to focus on relaxation, understanding that everything around me did not have to be in turmoil. I learned how to use my inner sense of calm to function on a regular basis, just from hearing her tone of voice.

During one of my visits, Melissa and I talked about moments I was embarrassed about. The one that came to mind was when I discovered Lynette was researching depression and the brain, perhaps for a school project. I felt embarrassed when I saw the information that she worked on, because I could only link her project to my situation, disorder, mood swings, and behaviors. I explained to Melissa, although I saw it by chance, I believe this project brought some clarity to me. I used this information to put some action into my Live Health habits, in this case, to recognize depression and its effect on the brain. This data helped me understand more about the condition, symptoms, and treatments, which were all important to know.

Melissa also asked me to tell her more about another subject that was embarrassing to me: my relationship with my children and their reactions to my outbursts and erratic behaviors. I told her that my sons got used to my outbursts; however, my oldest son, Mike Jr. either walked away and ignored me, or get physical when I was in a rage because I believed he was disrespectful to me. My other son Patrick just ignored me when my outbursts happened, but he would later question me about my actions. Lynette had a plan to fix me, at least that's what I thought when she started her pre-medical education at the University of Michigan. Another embarrassing moment that I spoke with Melissa about was how I dealt with my hidden struggles of facing bankruptcy while Lynette was in college, Patrick desired to go to a media art school, and Mike Jr. had ambitions for culinary arts and hoped to become a chef one day. I kept my financial struggles to myself, secretly worried that they would not be able to fulfill their dreams and ambitions. This financial struggle alone made it important for me to have a Know Money habit, in order to take control over my

Chapter 4: But, Habits Don't Lie

broken-down financial disaster before it was impossible to recover.

I also had to work hard to overcome my disorder and put the prescription drugs behind me, so I could make a strong comeback from the mistakes I made with my family, marriage, and finances. In 2005, I really got to celebrate a win over defeating my depression and bipolar disorder, by not having to take any more medication. I continued therapy for a while longer with Melissa, and we often talked about some of the steps that I felt worked to get off medication. Physical exercise, drinking lots of water, embracing my spiritual health in the mornings, tuning out negativity with my daily positive affirmations were all useful for my recovery. My own habits to overcome obstacles in order to win are:

1. Visualize Faith
2. Be Real
3. Target Success
4. Know Money
5. Live Health
6. Just Win
7. Think Repeat

This study of my habits was from my own research into my journey, but life was not instantly a breeze; I had many wins in my life, yet I recognized that I was still a top-level candidate for relapse. My job at the DPS was eliminated because of restructuring, so once again, I was without a job. But I built so much confidence in my quality skills as a career financial auditor, fraud examiner, and licensed builder, that I began to research and work on the start-up of a consulting business.

When I struggled through my disorder, I talked to Mama from time to time about the feelings and symptoms I experienced. Just like Mama, she said, "The best way is to first handle it with prayer." Although she wanted to see my relationship with my children and Angie get better, she knew through our discussions that it would be up to me to find ways to make that reconciliation happen. She reminded me that she had the confidence in me to find my own answers to happiness. Mama, in her wise way pointed out, that it matters less about *what* we do, than about *how* we do it that makes the difference in our lives. Mama remarried after divorcing my father after 24 years of marriage. And since I had been married for 25 years to Angie, Mama didn't have to understand what we were going through; she just wanted to prevent us from divorcing after so many years of marriage.

Mama always had monthly dinner dates with each of her children living in Detroit or those who might be visiting. My special day for our dinner was on Wednesday, and these dates often included her husband Garrett. We started out with some catch-up discussions and talking about world events. But, the after-dinner conversations that we had, sometimes got deep. One time, Mama reminded me about the serious struggles my sister Sharon had with her mental health, about how she wanted to move back to Detroit. Mama asked if I could just spend some time listening to Sharon, even if I didn't take any action; just listen. Mama also told me how proud she was that I defeated my disorder, though I had tried to hide it from her because I didn't want her to be concerned about me.

I did end up granting Mama's wish to connect with Sharon and to be a listening ear, although I had already contacted Sharon about her struggles. I told her how I defeated my disorder and obstacles with effective habits that I used to guide my life. I was interested in sharing with her how I did it. It's important to be in a position to help someone, even when facing something that is really hard, like working with a challenged relative who needs a lot of love and support. Sharon sound excited that I was willing to help her, and I was glad that since overcoming my disorder, I once again found a desire to help others through obstacles.

After three months, I began to realize that my unemployment payment benefits were running out. Out of work, with some of my business revenues left over, I finally made the bold decision to start a financial consulting business, so I could enjoy the benefits of freedom and working for myself again. I was fortunate to gain contracts with a CPA firm and a law firm, for my financial and auditing services, and I worked as an expert in fraud prevention for various individuals and a non-profit organization.

As the year went by, I got so busy with consulting that I missed out on my dinner dates with Mama. I felt bad that I had become too busy to visit. In April 2007, Mama called me to remind me about my brother Calvin's birthday, and our need to catch up, since we had not talked in a while. She told me she had been under the weather and the sound of her raspy voice was evidence that something was going on. She also told me that she had not gone on walks with her husband Garrett in a while because she didn't feel up to it. I paid close attention to her, because it seemed like she had a bad cold that she could not shake loose. Ten days later, Mama was admitted into the hospital.

During the first few days as the doctors tried to find out what was going on with her, Mama, however, wanted to know how things were going with Angie and me, as I worked hard through my recovery. I explained to Mama, that sometimes the low energy that we had in our marriage was just our feelings of unworthiness to each other because we weren't trying to rebuild. It was sometimes hard to stay in the marriage because we both did and said things that were hurtful to each other, that we wished we could take back. We had to accept who we were to each other, which did not feel like the loving couple that we portrayed to others, with the fake smiles and the appearance of happiness that only caused a buildup of uncontrollable stress. Mama just laid there in the bed and quietly pondered my explanations. I wasn't sure if she agreed with how I saw my marriage and

Chapter 4: But, Habits Don't Lie

where we were headed, but she did give me the wisdom to keep praying on it, because prayer is the answer. Since I did pray, I took her advice, seeking for the answers.

A day or so after my discussion, Mama started having more trouble breathing, so much that they had to put her on a ventilator. Mama never regained consciousness from then on. The family was called in, and the doctors told us that Mama's prognosis was pulmonary lung disease. They also said she would only have about three to five days to live. We sat around the room in silence for a few moments, processing the doctor's prognosis. Although we did not accept the defeat, it was a sad day for us. Two days after we got the news, on May 8, 2007, Mama passed away.

As I sat in her quiet hospital room where Mama laid, looking like an angel sleeping. I took a moment to reminisce about the many things she said, one of them was that I was named after Michael the "Angel", and as my tears slowly came, I couldn't help but to have a little chuckle inside, hearing my father once say, " boy, your mama got her Michael's all mixed up, because you were named after your uncle Michael". I also thought about the many characteristics Mama said she admired in me, like my confidence and my willingness to help others. Her support directed me to act right and to be good to myself and others, no matter what the environment was. I learned how to live a peaceful life, and I was determined to take some pages from Mama's life story. She always said, "Things happen for a reason," and "Worrying is a needless occupation" which continues to always be my pick-me-up to this day. This statement gave me the strength to continue whatever I started. Through my life journey and through growing up, Mama made sure that she gave me a thought, a prayer, or advice on a habit that I should pay attention to. In her peace, I know I will always hear her voice telling me, "Always keep prayer first. "That was Mama!

"Expecting the best of yourself will keep you going even when difficult challenges try to block your way."

~Les Brown

Up Thoughts for Down Times

To seek clarity, I realized that I had to go through a process of life energy flows to rebound from some difficulties, and struggles. I was disappointed in myself, but in a decision to move on from my marriage situation, I had to accept the only possible way to be happy was to terminate my 27-year marriage. This divorce was yet another loss in my life, especially after Mama's passing. Divorce, in every way, was not an easy or pleasant process. Memories of the good times would always exist;

Chapter 4: But, Habits Don't Lie

however, the unresolved feelings and issues took longer to heal. The ability to communicate for the betterment of our friends and family was possible because, Angie and I were able to keep the lines of communication open, as we continued to support each other and look for the best for our children. Our children agreed that divorce was the best decision for us to make, and they gave us their blessings, which helped us to heal.

I was finally free, yet unsure of how to move on. I began to think about a connection with a like-minded person who would save me from heartbreak, rejection, and judgement. I did not want to be alone, without a soulmate, because I really enjoy connecting with and savoring life together with another person. Sometimes you can be around someone you connect with, and you won't even know it until you start asking the right questions. I was in the right place at the right time, when my friend Marlowe, introduced me to his business partner Joyce, at one of their monthly meetings. Over time we came to appreciate each other. She recognized me for who I was, and not who I wanted to be. In only a matter of time, our deep discussions turned into love; she was my soulmate and the love of my life. Joyce and I got married on August 2, 2008. Every day since, I have enjoyed my life mission to make her happy by starting and ending each day in love. I knew, as I continued to follow my habits, that this love that I found was what I needed to reclaim my life. Joyce and I love spending time on so many things together like with our families, planning vacations, special events, and just being around each other. Both of us enjoy keeping up with our siblings, and we had the chance to really get to know them.

One of the pledges that my siblings and I made to Mama before she passed away, was to look out for each other. My brother Sandy, who was a karate expert and in good physical shape, had to have a hip operation a few days after my wedding to Joyce. The surgery must have gone wrong, because a couple days later he had to return to the hospital emergency room, complaining about pain. After being in the ER for a short time, they gave him a valium and sent him home to rest. Two days later, when Sandy woke up in the morning, his body was in a quadriplegic state, with very little movement. We were shocked at how quickly his body failed. At the age of 52, Sandy passed away from septic shock on October 16, 2008. This situation was difficult to deal with so soon after Mama's death. While the hospital staff prepared his body for the morgue, I went outside to sit on a fence and get some air. I stared up in the sky, trying to gain some understanding about what happened so swiftly and the events leading up to his death. My sorrow and grief were an inevitable part of life, and I knew I had to find a way to cope with this tragedy.

I took time off after Sandy's passing, but eventually, I had to go back to work, yet several negative situations had an impact on my business. The growing number of deficit districts was a political nightmare for many of the school districts, because emergency managers had to take control of the operations. The politics and the operations of each district had a big impact on how we got paid. As time went on, I was not as successful as I wanted to be in my consulting business. Every day, I recognized my victory in overcoming my disorder, yet I failed to accept or even recognize that I was drowning in debt from my ambition to build a stronger business.

As visionaries, we must never lose sight of the dreams to come, but by making the necessary adjustments to align those opportunities and ambitions, we may have to find another route to get to our dreams. So, when the Michigan Department of Education made me an offer to work as a fiscal monitor, I accepted the job to acquire some steady income. With this new position, I worked in a program finance office as a monitor instead of an auditor. I was also fortunate to meet my co-worker Nancy Jo, who came to our office a few months before me, from the Michigan Auditor General office. In a short time, Nancy Jo and I, who were responsible for monitoring the entire state of Michigan, became good friends.

During the first year of working in the office, I still had to commute from the Detroit area to Lansing when I was not in the field. When my job required overnight stays at the hotel, I spent a lot of time on the telephone in the evenings talking with my sister Sharon. Six months after

Sandy's death, she had still not gotten over the loss, and she dealt with several medical issues, as well. Sharon had a disorder that was complex, and each time I spoke with her, I had to be patient. Each time we spoke, she felt it was my responsibility to help her move back to Detroit. She depended on my immediate actions because she said I listened to her. During one phone conversation, I finally got her to calm down enough to listen to my offer to give suggestions to improve her health, and she accepted. In no way did I recommend for her to stop seeing her health professionals, and I made it clear that I would only help her with some habits to assist her in getting better. We talked about Visualize Faith and Living Healthy during that discussion.

I was amazed and happy at her first steps in trying. I approached the process so that she could see herself as a winner, and I could feel the positive energy around her. We started with Habit One: Visualize Faith, and I was able to give her some assignments as we communicated by telephone. I reminded her how Mama used to read the Bible at night and encouraged us all to do the same. We started just speaking about Mama's faith and how Sharon could Visualize Faith in her own life.

After five weeks of Sunday calls, we had many discussions about certain Bible verses that she wanted to challenge me on, or I talked about being motivated. I shared with her quotes from some of my favorite female motivational speakers like Lisa Nichols, Joyce Meyer,

Chapter 4: But, Habits Don't Lie

and Iyania Vanzant to help her get pumped up for more positive talk. Once I got her in a consistent positive mood, I related it to her faith and how she was improving. Sharon also talked about getting back in shape, and she made healthy living another one of her goals. I decided to take a slow approach with her training because she was making new discoveries, and I didn't want to discourage her with a faster pace.

On one particular Sunday, Sharon called me, but she didn't sound like that same happy person with the spirit of improvement that she had during our previous call. She refused to go into much detail, other than saying everything was all right. The next week, Sharon did not call me, and I became nervous, but I hoped she was just busy with her new job. Days later I found out from my father that Sharon was missing. When I got the news, I didn't want to process what missing was supposed to mean. I kept my faith and prayed for her safe return home, but on August 15, 2010, I received a call at work from the Kansas City Police, informing me that they found my sister dead, underneath a blanket in the back seat of her car, where she committed suicide. When they told me Sharon was deceased, I just lost it while in my office.

Comfort came from Eleanor, the Director of Special Education and my Supervisor John, who knelt and prayed with me. Eleanor stopped what she was doing and cleared her calendar for the day, just to take me home, which was 100 miles away. As we drove, she provided a spiritual presence that I needed most of all. Rethinking the moments that led up to discovering that my beautiful and sweet sister committed suicide was a nightmare that I just couldn't wish away. I knew I had to be strong to comfort her children in this time of sorrow. Through all the support from family and friends, we had to accept what happened and the reality of losing another sibling.

The support of my friends like Stratford, who told me to stay strong in prayer, Nancy Jo, who reminded me that I had to reinvent myself for the better, and Jeff, who always reminded me to repeat what works, made my healing process so much better. I had no choice but to fight my hardest to avoid a relapse, so that I would not become a victim to that ugly disorder again. As I remembered how I overcame my obstacles, I knew I would never be immune from having challenges, from dealing with grief or set-backs, or from losing people really close to me. My cousin Ebbie, who taught me the ins-and-outs of the Business "Hustle" in the real world, left this earth younger than 60 years of age. And while writing this book my father passed away quietly, a few days after his 85th birthday. I still deal with people and business hiccups, and even near-death experiences as I travel through this forever-changing world.

So, I'm grateful to share the moments when I grew in my self-image and responsibility, with the choices that I had. My willingness to know that I had to readjust my game plans for better opportunities yet conquer fear and surrender to courage in the process, helped me walk with a changed attitude. These life experiences meant that I needed to really embrace those habits that got me through this life. Not only did I find a way to take control of my life by using habits that worked, I continue to research how habits can pull you through any obstacle or mental and emotional wreckage.

"Faith is taking the first step even when you don't see the whole staircase."

~Martin Luther King, Jr.

Habit One: Visualize Faith

In Prayer and Meditation, Is Freedom

The Visualize Faith habit is powerful because it speaks to your actions to overcome obstacles or doubt. This habit reminds you about the importance of daily prayer and meditation to seek mental relaxation. When you set your intentions to pray and meditate, you are supposed to let go of all your grudges and emotions in order to receive that desired victory. What I also discovered through my journey to healing is that once you use this Visualize Faith habit, you won't have time for doubt.

I gratefully accepted the teaching of the late Dr. Herbert B. Robinson, Sr., the Pastor of the church where I attended since I was a child. He challenged the congregation weekly with the precious passage of Proverbs 3:5-6. *"Trust in the Lord with all thine heart; and lean not unto thine own understanding. In all thy ways acknowledge Him, and He shall direct thy paths."* The words speak for themselves that we are to trust and acknowledge the Lord. Our church still stands on this passage as our prayer, under the leadership of his son, Dr. Herbert B. Robinson, Jr.

Each time I succumb to my fears, whether completing an educational or personal goal, dealing with racial tension, losing employment, struggling in marriage, managing my disorder, or grieving, I think of these words of healing prayer from my Pastor and Mama. Through every tear-soaked moment, I had to find my way back to understanding the importance of daily praying and meditation, because if I didn't, I felt lost. This daily practice gave me freedom from stress, depression, tension, pain, and sorrow by conquering fear through prayer.

Prayer helped me build a firm foundation in my faith to get well, be strong, and win! So, it was my duty to Visualize Faith as a powerful habit for consistency. My intentional reflection gave me lasting peace when I meditated, and it invited happiness into my life. I meditated each morning in a private space and sometimes in the evenings with a group, as I learned how to set my intentions for a positive outcome.

My mission to create a Visualize Faith habit also included my daily affirmation, "Say It and Believe It." I capture an area of myself that I need to work on or an area in my life where I might need support. Then, I verbalize affirmations like, "I am aware that my current situation is not forever," "I am proud of myself," or "I exercise and move daily." As I grew out of my disorder, I had to have enough confidence to believe in myself. Affirmations may not work for everyone; however, they do for me.

Actually, it is the process of learning how to capture the affirmations that will help you grow. I had to really stand strong in my faith, so my affirmations spoke to move me forward and defeat my obstacles. Another one of my faith and confidence affirmations is, "Since I was given this day to win, I choose to remain calm, relaxed, and happy all day." To achieve progress from affirmations, use a goal-related action that you want to achieve results in. Repeat this affirmation until it becomes a natural part of your life. Daily affirmations changed my mindset so that I was open to make changes and reach my goals.

> *"Everything you want is on the other side of fear."*
>
> ~Jack Canfield

To Be Fearless and Never Quit

My discovery of speakers like Les Brown, Tony Robbins, Brian Tracy, as well as my accounting instructor Dallas, motivated and helped me to keep my confidence level up and receive the guidance to be fearless, be strong, and be unstoppable. These motivational teachers impacted my life even before I found out about my depression and bipolar disorder. Their teachings helped me to rise from every moment of shame and the feeling of failure. When I dipped to a low point, I often sharpened my focus back on, *"When your why is big enough, you will find your how,"* that I learned from Les Brown's spoken words of encouragement. I became mentally stronger with confidence and determination.

"Determination is the wake-up call to the human will," as Tony Robbins expressed in his book, *Awaken the Giant*. These statements gave me the determination and strength to continue my journey from my obstacles to recovery.

Listening to a quote or a thought from a motivational speaker was a connection for me because these speakers gave me the drive and determination to focus on particular areas of my life to lift me when I was down. During my journey to write this book, I was fortunate to meet another one of my favorite motivational and inspirational speakers, Lisa Nichols, at a "Motivating the Masses" four-day conference in Atlanta. There, I had a major breakthrough.

I arrived in Atlanta on November 1, 2017, and I was excited about being among like-minded people. But, I had a hidden sadness inside me that I could not shake loose for the past seven years. November 1st was Sharon's birthday, and each year on that day, I still mourned her loss and wondered what more could I have done to keep her grounded. During an exercise session at the conference, Lisa Nichols demanded that we find and connect with our "Earth Angels," so we could release those things that were holding us down, like achieving our goals, ambitions, and having faith.

We broke up into groups of four and surrounded each person individually to give them love, support, and the space that was necessary for them to feel their

Chapter 5: Habit One: Visualize Faith

breakthrough happening. Our own powerful voices, through repeating an affirmation or making a commitment for an improvement, was the manifestation for our breakthrough. I am so grateful for Lisa Nichols and my Earth Angels: Renee Smith, Darnelle Parker, and Toi Rutherford who were there to witness, comfort, and confirm my breakthrough, as I visualized my faith to be "Fearless, Strong, and Brave."

Allow the Memories to Live On

Memories can cheer you up and help you grow, yet they can sometimes bring you down. However, memories are always a part of our lives. I am forever challenged to have many of my own memories connected only with pictures in my mind. Just like that, I woke up one day, expecting a happy day, only to have that hope change within a few hours. I discovered that a leaky pipe ruined year of photographs that I had organized in chronological order, from my three-year-old childhood to some of my most current events.

Yep, just like that, I lost hundreds of pictures and memories as they lay organized on my pool table, waiting, while that leaky pipe went drip-drip-drip for days unnoticed. This disaster first reminded me of the many memories that I wouldn't be able to see again. I felt disappointed in myself because I had not taken the necessary action to protect the pictures. So many times, I had told myself that I needed to move these pictures back into the albums and boxes where they came from.

The photos I lost showed some of the priceless pictured memories of my sister Sharon and me, but the water damage changed them into a faded vision, and our faces appeared as a cloud. In that moment of shock, when I realized my photos were irreparable, I discovered that the memories of my loved ones were not lost.

Sometimes, we welcome a space for the memories, and sometimes they catch us off guard, tease us, and bring up some of the things that may hurt us or give us peace, as we picture the expression of happiness in our moments of vulnerability. Don't rebuke being stuck or lost in your memories, whether good or bad. We must recognize how blessed we are to have remembrances from childhood and the opportunity to be in a place to have memories.

Visualize Faith helped me to be positive with this loss, as I transformed from having to physically see pictures in order to strengthen my memories, to visualizing past moments and allowing the mental memories to live on. *"Most things are forgotten over time. Even the war itself, the life-and-death struggle people went through is now like something from the distant past. We're so caught up in our everyday lives that events of the past are no longer in orbit around our minds. There are just too many things we have to think about every day, too many new things we have to learn. But still, no matter how much time passes, no matter what takes place in the interim, there are some things we can never assign to oblivion, memories we can never rub away. They remain with us forever, like a touchstone."* ~ Haruki Murakami

Coach "Win" Action Steps:

Can you identify with Visualize Faith as a habit?

Sometimes we grow accustomed to certain habits, but we don't really notice how they impact us on a daily basis until they have been tried and tested. Our habits can have a profound influence on the way we look at life, the way we carry ourselves, the way we conduct our thoughts, and the way we speak and express the words that come from our mouth. Don't settle for a life where you empower the negative habits and weaken the positive habits that you need in your life. Start with the vision of faith. *Write down your schedule for daily prayer and meditation*:

Write down at least 5 powerful affirmations and the intentions that you will live by daily:

Write down the method you will use to release your bad memories and how you will allow the good memories to live on:

Write down 3 actions items that will empower you to be Fear-Less, Strong, and Unstoppable:

"Everything will line up perfectly when knowing and living the truth becomes more important than looking good."

~Alan Cohen

Habit Two: "Be Real"

Living an Authentic Life

Be Real is a practical habit about being authentic. Growing up, I always saw Mama as one of the most authentic people I knew because she was always the same "real" person whenever you saw her. Even during some of the toughest times we experienced, Mama always flashed a smile then found a positive outcome or lesson while processing her thoughts for a solution or conclusion. In the case of my siblings and me, this solution was often a reward or a punishment she gave in love. She reminded us to always be honest with people about who we were and what we wanted.

As I found my way through recovery from my disorder, I knew of many suggestions Mama advised me on, but sometimes they fell on deaf ears. I recognized quickly how accustomed I became to hiding my true feelings about who I was. In doing so, I found I was comfortable playing a fake person to bury what was really bothering me. As I searched for habits to exercise as a daily routine and incorporate in my arsenal for recovery, I knew I just had to Be Real.

In 2002, I was fortunate to meet Norma Hollis who ran training programs for public speakers. At the time, I was a volunteer with the Accounting Aid Society as an income tax preparer but desired to move into the Financial Literacy program, which required me to speak to many individuals and groups about financial literacy. I wanted to become a better speaker, so I enrolled in Norma's "Process to Become a Professional Speaker" series. I enjoyed helping people as part of my remedy for getting well from my disorder, and the process of becoming a professional speaker really helped me reach my audience. Through the presentations I gave as part of the program and my consulting business, I became successful speaking as a Certified Financial Literacy Trainer.

Because of my speaking success, in 2006, I was the recipient of the Outstanding Financial Literacy Award from the Michigan Accounting Aid Society. This award was an honor and a significant tool that allowed me to use my upbringing and social skills to help others, which played a unique part in their lives and in mine. When I spoke at various places with my serious statements, emotional expressions, or concerned thoughts, I used my Be Real habit to show my authentic voice and speaking skill so that I was able to reach many people.

I was grateful for the training that helped me develop and improve my speaking skills, so I began researching authenticity and how your inner nature and outer voice are connected to how you portray yourself to others. As far as authenticity, good or bad, it is important to know people for who they are. Working on myself was a rewarding experience for me, and I learned to make a habit of being authentic.

Through the process of using my true voice, I brought awareness, integrity, motivation, and inspiration to those attending my speaking engagements. I kept my connection with Norma Hollis, and after becoming a more focused speaker, I continued to look for something new and different. I became a certified authenticity coach through her Authenticity U program. A link is provided for you to take an authenticity assessment in the action steps below.

Make Peace, Forgive, Love, and Go Forward

To be authentic, consistent and true to myself, I had to make peace, forgive, love more, and move forward. I was able to do this by releasing my bad feelings or thoughts about those who may have harmed me or my family; I gave forgiveness to both them and me. There were many people who I needed to apologize to or give forgiveness. But in particular, I wanted to express to Angie my sincere apology of how I treated her throughout our struggles, as well as my forgiveness of her. I was able to breathe again after I expressed my remorse. Letting go of the hurt created an end to the emotional pains from our marriage.

Many times, the physical discomfort in our body is about the inner pain that causes the suffering. Regret for something you did, that is worthy of an apology, could cause you to drag the weight of the past wherever you go, until you release it. Regret will also drain your energy, leaving you less available for the present activities you look forward to, because you constantly feed on the past for the "when," the "how," and the "why" previous events happened.

Forgiving doesn't always heal the bitter past, but it may heal some of the emotional pain. I found out that forgiveness is the highest and most beautiful form of love and peace you can offer because it allows you to go forward by taking the energy you lost through regret and turning it into something positive and constructive. When you tell someone that you are sorry, leave the apology at that, because you don't always need to explain a sorry, especially if you know it's your fault. By apologizing, you already accepted the fault in the situation, and you should genuinely own your remorse with that seal of apology.

Have Integrity, Lead, and Inspire Someone

Integrity is a belief system of being honest with others and adhering to high moral standards. After pulling myself up from being down for so long, I had to rebuild my circumstances with new relationships that would help me achieve my goals. To Be Real in building new personal and professional relationships, I wanted my integrity to show as a strong foundation of commitment, self-trust, faith, and authenticity in everything I did. When you act with integrity, your family, colleagues, staff, and customers will place their trust in you. However, as humans, we go through changes, we have set-backs, or may fail from time to time, but it does not always mean that you have lost your integrity.

Making an adjustment or improvement to your integrity is one of the greatest signs of strength you can have, because you recognize that integrity takes a lifetime to build, but only a moment to lose. When you manage your integrity, you can lead people, because character is powerful. We often look at leaders to be the people up front to lead, but we forget about those who lead from behind, who are in many cases even more equipped to lead. When a person leads from behind, they are able to step forward in key moments to enable innovation. The process to overcome obstacles in a leadership role takes some patience, because good leaders remain committed, regardless of the situation. They are always looking for new ideas, insight, and information. The highest compliment received by a leader, is one that is given by the individuals who follow them.

You are obligated to inspire and to Be Real for those who follow you or the people who look up to you. As I came out of my depression, I wanted to be around people who motivated me, as well as those I could inspire. I connected with inspirational people, like my authenticity

Habits Don't Lie

coach Norma, who provided me with so many wonderful tools and resources to connect authenticity with integrity, leadership, and inspiration. I also continued my training in authenticity, motivation, and inspiration, as I related with speakers like Zig Ziglar, Les Brown, Lisa Nichols, Jack Canfield, and Tony Robbins.

Through all my self-taught learning and training, I was able to identify the Be Real habit for my transformation to becoming a much happier person. I encourage you to use the Be Real habit to inspire someone each and every day.

Coach "Win" Action Steps:

Go to: www.authenthenticityassessment.com and take your free authenticity assessment. Follow the instructions on how to read your score and future scores for the best benefit. *In the space below, write down your thoughts about your first assessment:*

Write down at least 5 people that you either need to make peace with, apologize to, or forgive, so you can go forward. Also identify what you have released through this experience:

Having integrity is a habit. For example, when you keep your word and deliver on your promises, people will trust you, and this can build strong relationships. How does integrity show up in your life?

"A good leader is a person who takes a little more than his share of the blame and a little less than his share of the credit." ~ John Maxwell

How would you lead from behind?

Inspiration is the greatest gift that you can give someone. How do you inspire others? *Complete the sentences below:*

I inspire people every day with a:

I inspire people by telling them:

I inspire others by caring:

I inspire others by expecting:

I inspire others by being:

"SUCCESS leaves CLUES!"

~Tony Robbins

Habit Three: "Target Success"

Passion, Purpose, and Accountability

Target Success determines your target audience, which means you need to have focus. As a young person, I had an eagerness and willingness to work wherever I could get a job, so I learned my work ethic by taking multiple jobs to help my father and mother with expenses. However, as I got older, I lost the balance in my life by taking on too many opportunities before knowing what audience I served. My passion grew into my desire to have multiple careers; however, I did not serve my purpose and I was not always accountable for not meeting my goals. Although these opportunities gave me a great vision for multiple streams of income, they were the main contributors to my depression disorder, because I lost balance trying to accomplish too much at one time.

I selected this Target Success habit to redefine my purpose. I identify and understand that overworking wasn't just about achieving my goals to serve. Instead, I had to take my passion and re-focus it back to serving my audience separately for coaching and speaking, since my audience sometimes requested consulting or other services when available. This focus allowed me to be more creative in my business by guiding my clients to

Chapter 7: Habit Three: Target Success

become successful through a process of working smarter and not harder.

Target Success requires you to be accountable in order to achieve your goals through opportunities or business. Throughout my recovery, I had to be accountable for where I missed out, messed up, or just ignored the things that were important to me, as I worked and ran my home businesses. Trying to justify my downfalls with excuses made matters worse; however, once I kept my focus on my purpose, the excuses that I made for myself faded away, and I became more accountable for my actions and my choices.

Greatness, Planning, and Development

Many times, Mama told us to recognize our greatness and God-given talents. Most of the sweat and tears I shed to transform myself were actually for those people pulling for me to be successful. I had to embrace my greatness so that I would be able to follow a Target Success habit, which meant whenever I was down or depressed, I had to snap out of it.

Target Success forced me to take on a habit to read more professional-development books and articles. I began to read at least one book a month, even if I read the same book over in another month. One of the favorite books I read was, *What Makes The Great, Great,* by Dr. Dennis P. Kimbro, Ph.D. Dr. Kimbro's book outlines the strategies for extraordinary achievements, and he revealed powerful action lessons, which I carefully considered, in order to create my desired results of having flexible time, connections, and extra money by running a successful business.

This information came at an important time, because I needed a plan to pull me away from my convenient excuse to soak in the feeling of hopelessness; a far cry from the "Kingship" I once claimed as a child on the back-stairs at Mama Hushie's house. Dr. Kimbro's book of practical advice gave me the tools and inspiration to discover the power within myself. Through my efforts with a Target Success habit, I claimed my greatness!

"Some are born great, some achieve greatness, and some have greatness thrust upon them."

~ William Shakespeare

In planning my strategies to rise into my Target Success, I had to make changes in my actions. This strategic plan allowed me to achieve my new-found goals to organize a personal and business system for success, and to recognize the time necessary for research and development. Personal development was a great tool for encouragement and direction, but my adjustment came

Chapter 7: Habit Three: Target Success

through really understanding the what, the why, and the want for achieving my goals.

I had to be realistic in striving to make my goals attainable, by identifying the pros and cons over time that included a vision, support, and agreement with my spouse. I had to plan ahead by not waiting until the last minute, which meant that sometimes I had to say, "No," and mean it, so that I could reserve my "Yes," for better situations that came with proper time-management. I focused on following and tracking all of my progress, but in order to Target Success and follow through, I had to track each of my short-term goals, and identify every small accomplishment to stay motivated.

Power of Relationships and Fulfillment

Through my recovery, I learned that I don't have to be perfect to be lovable. This reason is why I value the power of relationships. When I look at those individuals who directly or indirectly helped me with a thought, guidance, or many prayers, I realize that they gave me a better understanding of personal and business relationships. In most personal relationships, we express our true feelings by having a deep personal connection. However, business can also be personal if we are willing to be part of a team and consider the benefits that come with business relationships. We feel more connected with the style of a person, their honesty, humanity, and loving spirit in both personal and business relationships. In our work or places of business, we Target Success by measuring or analyzing the outcomes. Yet, true fulfillment means having a good brand, reputation, drive, or determination to achieve successful outcomes.

Where love, seriousness, commitment, and spiritual relationships are important, cultivating fulfillment is still necessary and worthwhile. Before my commitment to remarry, I had to have an understanding with myself on what habits I needed to sustain this new relationship. In order to Target Success in my marriage, I had to strengthen my listening and communication skills to gain support for both my personal and business dreams and goals as we grew together. As I often tweaked the habits I used to help me achieve my goals, I identified the routines that I was comfortable with or I made the necessary adjustments. In my second marriage, I quickly found out that Joyce's fulfilment was not just the gifts, trips, or wining and dining that came with the routine, "Allow me to impress you, Honey" stage, although she did enjoy them. Instead, I learned that simple gifts and small gestures, like writing her love letters or leaving her flowers at home or work, put a bigger smile on her face. I discovered that I could never leave the house in the morning, afternoon, or evening without giving her a "See you later" kiss, and she did the same in exchange. These small tokens of affection became a new habit for me to strengthen my relationship.

This Target Success habit also allows me to really listen and focus on what is said, before I process the information into action. Through my recovery journey, I was able to listen and learn from many individuals, including those who shared personal and private conversations in a group session. In my group sessions, I was truly grateful to be among individuals that came from all walks of life. Many of them provided so much insight into their situations and how they managed or adjusted to find recovery. Through the strong support and assessments that came from the group sessions, I began to understand the importance of attending meetings in order to Target Success. In an environment of like-minded people that hold you accountable for your own goals, finding new strategies to overcome obstacles is possible. Because of my successful experience with group sessions, I did not hesitate to find out more about joining a Mastermind group that was once offered during a Mega Book Marketing University event in Los Angeles, hosted by Mark Hansen and Jack Canfield. I realized that by meeting those highly motivated people that shared my common goals, we could help improve each other.

"As soon as healing takes place, go out and heal somebody else."

~Maya Angelou

Coach "Win" Action Steps:

Instead of recognizing that my purpose and passion should lead to my accountability, I had passion before knowing my purpose or creating accountability. *How do your Purpose, Passion, and Accountability show up?*

Write down at least 5 lessons or attributes that define your "Greatness."

A lifestyle system of daily, organized procedures is the best way to avoid costly and unnecessary professional fees. In many cases, a readiness plan is either missed, delayed, or forgotten about. *What does Planning, and Development look like to keep you accountable?*

Finding powerful relationships and lasting fulfillment requires work. *List 3 things that have helped you out in a personal or business relationship:*

List 3 things that would give that relationship lasting fulfilment:

"I believe that the power to make money is a gift from God"

~John D. Rockerfeller

Habit Four: "Know Money"

Financial Literacy, a Life Mission

The Know Money habit looks at financial literacy as a life mission, so you can take ownership of your future. Financial literacy is essential to help consumers understand how to manage money, as well as helping those who have to deal with failed money issues from the past.

During my recovery, I had to face the problems that I created because I forgot the habits I learned as a youth about earning and using my money wisely. I was lost, but I never gave up on learning this important lesson, because the Know Money habit provides the energy tools to transform your relationship with money and help you achieve financial independence and abundance. This independence is not always about the money, but it can be achieved by knowing and following basic money habits.

It is our duty and responsibility to know basic money habits as we live in this forever changing economy. Financial literacy is so powerful; yet, many surveys show that on average, the general public is financially illiterate. This statistic may sound harsh, but unfortunately it is true. The root of the problem is not hard to find, because a lot of people acquire their financial knowledge haphazardly or by trial and error. From my work experience, I know many employers express concern about their employees bringing financial problems to the workplace. And divorce often happens because of financial issues; some people avoid marriage for the same reasons. There are failed business relationships because of the lack of timely and responsible money management; and overall embarrassment for those who have the ability to earn a high scale income, but live paycheck to paycheck. This inability to manage money is a big challenge in obtaining success.

Despite the numerous well-intentioned efforts over the last few years to increase - knowledge about saving, recent surveys show that the average U.S. household owes over $16,000 in credit card debt, and the average college senior has $ 28,950 in student loans. About 78% of Americans still live from paycheck to paycheck. One of the greatest financial obstacles for many people is the lack of awareness concerning their mental and spiritual connection with their bank account and assets. We have only recently recognized the shortcomings in financial understanding, and that is why financial literacy should be a life mission for everyone.

Even though there are some public schools in this country that have a financial literacy curriculum for seniors, there is still a need to increase the awareness for financial literacy and eradicate one of the nation's financial problems where it starts: with our children and young adults. I believe the greater importance is to focus on making sure young people understand the principles of saving and investing for the future. This understanding will help them become financially prepared for retirement someday, as well as preserving their accumulated wealth. A financial literacy life mission can effectively and efficiently guide you through accomplishing your goals using the Know Money habit.

Requirements for building a successful business include having a strategic alliance with others who have been successful. In my work, I have also seen and worked with many people in top positions who ran businesses that involved financial responsibility; however, they seemed to be clueless about basic financial knowledge. Before speaking about an SBA loan, business incentives, income tax business structures, or acquisition of real estate, one should first be engaged with some of the common factors of basic financial literacy:

1. *Financial institutions* like banks and credit unions. Determine the reasons why you should keep your money in any of these institutions. Your relationship with a safe and convenient institution can provide you with future offers and services that may help your personal and business growth.

2. *The basics of borrowing* a loan or applying for credit. You need to know your capacity to meet payments; understand available capital or assets that can be used as collateral; determine if you have the character and responsibility to make payments on bills or debts.

3. *The true cost of credit* is knowing your credit limit, credit score, and your credit history. Be aware that credit cards have a downside, and that they encourage irresponsible people. Splurging on yourself is okay sometimes but know that when you use many department store credit cards, they usually have a higher interest rate. Therefore, that sale item purchase could cost you a lot more because of the interest rate.

4. *Money matters* when knowing how to keep track of your money. Budgeting is critical because you need to know where your money goes. Budgeting means you must track and review the money trail. Imagine if you were a CFO and did not know how the money was actually spent. A spending plan, or budget, is a plan for spending and saving money as you monitor your weekly, monthly, and quarterly comparison of what you earn (income and revenue) versus where your money goes (saving, household, or business expenses). This plan is a good place for taking control of your financial situation and to gain confidence for the

Chapter 8: Habit Four: Know Money

future. Go to: https://www.coachwin.com/coach-win-play-book to receive a valuable interactive budgeting tool.

5. *Pay yourself first* because this important step is part of building your financial future. Everyone is worthy of getting paid, although you should always carefully identify your wants versus your needs. Your purpose for making money should have an impact on what you will do with it after you earn it. Your current and future obligations are important, so you must be the judge of how you pay yourself first. However, saving tips for a robust future should include using direct deposit for your various saving instruments (i.e. 401K, Roth IRA, Saving Plus Club accounts, etc.). As your wants and needs are identified in your budget, this allows you to reward yourself and to take an effortless approach to put away the money that you need for your future personal and business goals.

6. *A loan to own* a house or car comes with the responsibility of understanding installment loan payments that are repaid in equal monthly payments for a specified period, usually several years. It is an important Know Money habit to understand the different lending concepts, like a Fixed-Rate Loan, which is a loan that has an interest rate that stays the same throughout the

life of the loan. A Variable-Rate Loan is a loan that is attached with an interest rate that might change during any period of the loan as stated in the loan agreement. The Annual Percentage Rate is a measure of the cost of your loan expressed as a yearly percentage rate.

Therefore, you must look for a financial planner, financial literacy trainer, accountant, income tax expert, business coach, or other professional financial advisor for this mission. That person should be authentic and understanding, have the financial experience on each level of business that you hope to accomplish, and they must be a person with integrity.

"Wisdom is the principal thing; therefore, get wisdom: and with all thy getting, get understanding."

~ Proverbs 4:7-8 (KJV)

Don't Let Your Dreams Bankrupt You

I remember the first time I wanted to go into business for myself. I watched the television commercials and read the many news and magazine articles about how to run my own business or create a home business. These advertisements portrayed a vision of becoming a self-made millionaire with little effort, and the success stories of these millionaires were always seen holding stacks of money. For me, trying out or having several businesses came with a cost. I followed the Know Money habit as one of the steps that I identified during my recovery and pledge to do better, especially after I found myself in a situation that I thought I would never be in. No one could have ever told me that without a gambling problem, drug addiction, or an out-of-control spending problem, that I would have to declare bankruptcy.

I did have all of the above addictions and a spending problem, though they did not reveal themselves in the typical manner. I worked as a casino auditor with oversight operational responsibility, so I wasn't one to risk losing my financial future in the casinos for a make-believe guarantee of winning a "Jackpot." However, I still gambled by making bad decisions to support my dreams and goals without thinking or caring about the impact these decisions would have on my family and their future. At one point, I had two children who were interested in attending college during the same time. In addition, we had other commitments that I was not focused on. Many of the important family expenses became secondary because I had an inner drive to gamble on my future that I couldn't explain. I knew what it would take to achieve my dreams; "Just watch me," was the attitude I had.

Likewise, my drug addiction was not an abuse of drugs; however, while on prescribed drugs for my disorder, I had an addiction to making important decisions while knowing that the drug's side-effects altered my thinking. I should have not engaged in business at the level I was in, especially during my dark days when I felt trapped and unable to access my dreams without feeling on edge. Yet, feeling trapped was an excuse for me to justify my poor financial decisions.

There was also a desire to spend money on stuff that I did not need, though in general I was considered "cheap," so cheap, I was told I could "squeeze the water out of a buffalo on a nickel." However, through this time of irresponsibility, I began buying multiple items for my home or business but found out later that I already had them. My behavior, influenced by a poor self-image, caused me to make bad decisions, even when I knew that my actions seemed crazy. Many of these bad decisions led to my bankruptcy.

People who allow their dreams to bankrupt them often fool themselves into thinking that they're making money when they're simply not, because they spend more than they earn. In fact, I know several people who refuse to take a temporary job to support themselves while building a business, but instead, live with no income to pay their expenses, in the hope that a new contract or a

Chapter 8: Habit Four: Know Money

quick business opportunity will magically save them. Bankruptcy should not be used as a way to fund your debt or to reset your bad spending habits. I have advised a few clients, on their second or third bankruptcy, who are still living with a powerful dream to survive on. I am the first person to tell someone that a bankruptcy is a path to a fresh start. But, by all means, avoid another bankruptcy by attending a Fresh Start program offered by the bankruptcy court and follow the steps designed to help you, so your new beginning is successful.

I made a habit to pay more attention to the needs of my family. I realized that if the Know Money habit was going to work in my recovery, I had to set goals for myself to transform my financial life. This habit allowed my children to have the opportunity to extend their educational dreams without worrying about if I would be able to support them.

If you commit to the Know Money habit, it will always be there for your fresh start as you rebound from losses, failed goals, obstacles, and bad decisions. As long as you identify your weakness and commit to the glory of redefining and reinventing your money story, you will expand your capacity to receive more, so that you can give more. The strength of this habit comes from making a deep commitment to change your thinking, so that you grow and develop your personal and business strategies for financial wealth and success.

Growth Plans for Multiple Streams of Income

As I justified the use of household funds to invest in my business, I thank God that I had enough sense during my disorder not to dip into my 401K investment, although I did have that desire. But after rethinking my money habits from my youth, I had to build a system around my spending and form a plan to live in control. With the Know Money habit, my dreams of making money did not stop, but I was challenged to continue to have multiple streams of income, while committing to a personal business plan that made sense. This plan included my efforts to rebuild the money lost from family commitments by preparing growth plans for both my personal and my business functions. As I looked back on my bad decisions and saw what I had done without a plan, I was encouraged to make a concerted effort to eliminate those ills, so that I could move forward.

Personal and business plans should be customized for your personal needs with your goals and objective to grow. Your business ambitions, goals, and objectives should speak for themselves. I researched many personal and business plans, because I wanted to display my efforts of hope, possibility, and the necessity of achieving my goals and objectives, in both my personal and business-growth plans. A personal growth plan is meant for a long, drawn-out, kitchen-table discussion with your family, committed to the growth and support of one another. This type of plan was the style I had as a youth, as I pitched in my small amount of money to help grow and improve the future of our family. Such a discussion with your family will really confirm that everyone is in agreement on their priorities.

A successful business plan, however, will take some time and a lot more effort to see the vision for short and long-term goals. Map out how this plan should accomplish your purpose and desire to run your business or businesses. This serious documentation will allow you to see the steps you must take to achieve the stages of progress when you follow and review this plan often. Your business plan should be documented, and you may need to follow up with financial experts. However, if you are capable of outlining a business growth plan before you take it to a financial expert, you should have these minimum items detailed in your plan:

1. Executive summary and company description that will explain what your company is about and why it will be successful
2. Trend or market analysis
3. Organization and management structure
4. Service and product line
5. Funding request
6. Financial projections
7. Growth of your company
8. Succession plan or exit strategy

I have coached several clients, who bragged about having three or four businesses. But when I determined if they had a business plan for each of those companies, they didn't have proper plans or financial information. Without a plan these businesses are, in most cases, are nothing more than a hobby because they are just not making money or breaking even. Your business plan should be reviewed often and updated when necessary. It should include the execution of a short-term, as well as a long-term plan, readily available to gain business opportunities and resources.

As you consider your growth plan for multiple streams of income, the Know Money habit recognizes the importance of growth through financial wellness and having a living legacy. The ability to invest in someone's future while you are living should be in the sight of your growth plans. Most of us only think of a legacy as the amount of money or property left behind to someone in a will or bequest. This type of legacy may be the type of help that a person greatly appreciates or grows from. However, there are others who are irresponsible and squander the true purpose when they receive such a gift from a legacy. Therefore, "Living a Legacy" has so much more value, because you can give or share your physical and spiritual gifts, as well as share your money or property, while you are still living. This living legacy allows you to see and experience the growth of your legacy.

Coach "Win" Action Steps:

Create 5 steps that will broaden your understanding of financial literacy (i.e. contacting a financial institution, reading a newsletter, taking a mini community course on budgeting, or finding a national strategy for financial literacy):

Design the life of your dreams and identify a plan with the financial goals and objectives to accomplish them:

`

Write down your Personal Growth Plan and identify the people who should be a part of the plan:

Write down a summary of your Business Growth Plan and describe how it will make you successful:

"I don't care how old I live! I just want to be living while I am living!"

~Jack LaLanne

Habit Five: "Live Health"

Yes, Health Awareness is the Key

The Live Health habit identifies the importance of understanding that your body is a temple and how necessary it is to stay healthy. This habit moved me to take actions to overcome my disorder. Through the support of my therapist Melissa and group therapy, I was strongly convinced to use certain key habits to keep me focused through my recovery. Live Health habits set the parameters in identifying the routines I needed in order to be successful in overcoming my disorder. Jack LaLanne once said, "Develop a positive attitude. Think and picture how amazing you are going to be. Visualize it." That quote inspired me to have more health awareness.

When thinking about my health, I felt obligated to experiment with the habits I developed including Visualize Faith, Be Real, Target Success, Know Money, Live Health, Just Win, and Think Repeat. These habits developed from focusing on my overall health, including mental, emotional, spiritual, and physical health.

Before transitioning into closure with my disorder, I had to begin a new phase in my life by recognizing and clarifying the symptoms and causes that left me trapped in my depression and bipolar disorder. As I read the information about depression that my daughter Lynette researched in an attempt to help me, I felt embarrassed because of the distance I felt between us. I imagined that my life-changing symptoms and episodes had an impact on her and led her to pursue pre-medical studies and receive her bachelor's degree in Brain, Behavior, and Cognitive Science. This information compelled me to think about my responsibility in understanding my depression and bipolar disorder as described in some of her work below:

Depression and the Brain

Depression is one of the most common psychological disorders in America, and only second as the most common chronic conditions encountered in general medical practice. Over 17 million Americans will experience depression each year but the amount of people suffering can never truly be determined. Depression is a disorder that is commonly confused with typical sadness or stress, but real clinical depression can alter the way you feel and think. Depression can also change your behavior and your physical well-being. It can last for weeks, months, or even years and can be experienced every day. Although depression is treatable, many suffer unknowingly due to their lack of understanding about the disorder.

Depression comes in many different types. The diagnosis of each type depends on the intensity, duration, and cause of symptoms. A type of depression that has to do with intensity is bipolar disorder. Bipolar disorder differs with moderate or major depression because it has presence of at least one manic episode. A manic episode is an abnormally elevated, expansive, or irritable mood, not related to substance abuse or medical condition that lasts for at least a week and includes disturbances in behavior and thinking that results in significant life adjustment problems.

With this helpful information, I honored the Live Health habit because my focus was on health recovery. Being open and willing to get better brought my dreams of recovery into reality.

> *"Your life does not get better by chance, it gets better by change."*
>
> ~Jim Rohn

Simplify a Health-Wellness Routine

Having good health is sometimes taken for granted until we get sick; then we start to reflect on a health-wellness plan after the fact. Health is a dynamic process because it is always changing. Growing up with asthma forced me to make adjustments so I could enjoy a life of sports.

One of those adjustments was to drink lots of water to keep my airways and body hydrated, which allowed me to run track, lift weights, swim, and play baseball and football. As an adult, I still drink about a gallon of water a day and continue a routine exercise program at least five times a week, including yoga, walking, and weight conditioning. Exercise makes me feel good, energizes me, and allows me to focus on the day better than when I am not active.

As we make a shift in our ages or lifestyles, our level of health may change. Good health is enjoyed because we feel fine, but when we get sick, we might not feel challenged until it becomes a serious illness. However, I believe we can improve our health on a daily basis with certain factors that influence our state of health wellness, including good nutrition, physical activity, stress-coping methods, positive relationships, and career choices. The Live Health habit is unique for simplifying a health-wellness and fitness regimen as follows:

1. Embrace your spiritual health
2. Set daily intentions to learn and grow mentally
3. Eat light in the morning, eat lunch according to appetite, and eat less in the evening
4. Drink plenty of water
5. Listen to your body
6. Schedule routine doctor, dentist, and other health-specialist appointments and follow-up visits
7. Commit to daily exercise

8. Control your weight
9. Indulge in pampering, pleasure, and happiness
10. Reset with relaxation and plenty of sleep

As a man, I am aware of the lack of care that many men have for themselves when it comes to health wellness. Health is a human right and responsibility, not a privilege. Unfortunately, when it comes to lifestyle, men are not judged by whether they are healthy, instead they are judged by whether they can contribute to the responsibilities of a household financially, physically, or through leadership.

As an authenticity coach, I also speak and teach about the importance of health wellness and fitness obedience so that individuals can be aware and support a Live Health habit. However, it seems like a Live Health habit is one of the most difficult habits to incorporate because I still can't do enough to encourage most individuals to complete the necessary physical activity on a regular basis.

The Live Health habit also helps you develop a good relationship with your doctor because many important health issues can only be detected when examined over time by a physician or health specialist. I was told as a young man, that if we make the right health decisions, like visiting a doctor at an early age and on a regular basis, this choice will make a difference over time by allowing us to manage and prevent health conditions instead of dealing later with serious medical events.

Monitoring should be consistent and at a minimum we should all be aware of:

- Weight and Body Mass Index (BMI)
- Oral Health
- Cardiovascular Health
- Lung and Respiratory System
- Blood Pressure
- Cholesterol
- Blood Glucose Levels
- Colorectal Cancer
- Sexual/Reproductive Health
- Calcium and Bone Density

A simplified health-wellness program can be developed for anyone. When you believe that you are ultimately in control of your health and how you feel, you will be empowered with the Live Health habit for daily support.

"A person cannot succeed in anything without a good, sound body...a body that is able to stand up against hardships, that is able to endure."

~ Booker T. Washington

Brain Food, Body Fuel, and Happy Rest

To have a successful day you must power up with positive habits. The Live Health habit focuses on many routines to include daily. Some of these habits should be done within the first few hours of waking up in order to be more productive. Benjamin Franklin said, "Early to bed and early to rise makes a man healthy, wealthy, and wise." I am still learning the importance of being well-rested. This pattern is still a work-in-progress for me, but I still choose good habits to start each day with:

- Wake up early for a good morning, it's 4:30 a.m. for me
- Have an 8 to 10-ounce drink of water, first thing in the morning
- Avoid TV or social media for the first two hours of the morning
- Pray and meditate for at least 15-20 minutes
- Exercise (yoga, stretching, or weight training) from 20-60 minutes, in the morning, evening, or both
- If you drink coffee, no more than 3 cups a day, but think about green tea too
- Tell at least 10 people before 9:30 a.m., "Good Morning," or "Hello," with a smile
- Eat three balanced meals with portions conducive to the time of day, that include vegetables, fruit, low-carbs, fiber, and protein, with or without meat

Chapter 9: Habit Five: Live Health

- Have a smoothie for an energy booster, at least five days a week, which may include various fruit, vegetables, or spices, depending on the day or workout
- Drink at least a gallon of water throughout the day, which is equivalent to eight 16.9-ounce water bottles
- Go to bed early enough for six to eight hours of sleep

Each day, in order to have peace with myself, I avoid negative talk, negative people and negative situations. There are more important opportunities that I look forward to. So, I end my day by mentally flushing out anything that isn't useful, peaceful, or joyful to me, which means I will be positive and ready for the next day.

I have learned how to pamper myself by either soaking my feet in warm vinegar water while listening to jazz music; find time to relax with a good book; take a nature walk with Joyce; or just laughing out loud at a funny movie or something that was said. I found that these practices allow me to Live Health!

"Sometimes you have to be willing to let go of something old to grab onto something new."

~ Lisa Nichols

Coach "Win" Action Steps:

Build a journal of your medical conditions and situations that you may have. *Write down at least five questions that you should ask your doctor and carefully document his or her answers or response. Your notes should include your physician information like their email address and phone number:*

Notes:

Physician Information:

Chapter 9: Habit Five: Live Health

Simplify your Health-Wellness plan with 7 "I Will" statements (i.e. I will monitor my blood pressure weekly), to monitor, control, and be aware of your health wellness:

How do you power up your day? Write down at least 8 things that you should do every day to be more productive:

"No matter how many mistakes you make or how slow you progress, you are still way ahead of everyone who isn't trying."

~Tony Robbins

Habit Six: "Just Win"

"Win-Win" Situation

The Just Win habit is my favorite habit because it focuses on the success caused by having a winning attitude. While becoming the man I am today, there were choices that I had to make, a mindset I searched for and fixed, and changes that I made to become a winner. I already celebrated my small wins by just being me.

With the Just Win habit, you are obligated to visualize an environment that is free of toxins, chaos, and negativity. You can praise small wins the same way you would celebrate a big win, and always think "Win-Win."

In Dr. Stephen R. Covey's book, *The 7 Habits of Highly Effective People*, Dr. Covey encourages each person to "Think Win-Win." He expressed that Win-Win is not a technique, but a total philosophy of human interactions where agreements or solutions are mutually beneficial and mutually satisfying. A Win-Win sees life as a cooperative area and not a competitive one. Therefore, both people get to eat the proverbial cake, and it will taste good!

Your excellence is not a skill, but your attitude is everything. To achieve winning results from your goals, overcome obstacles, or be selected for job promotions, you must be resilient and commit to a strong attitude for winning. The Just Win habit provides a bold and exciting perspective to challenge your thinking:

- Set a mission to accomplish
- Have the end in mind
- Use your willingness to get results
- Align with people who share your value
- Set time limits to stand by
- Have a habit to give more than required

The Just Win habit is my birthright and my connection with a Win-Win situation because of my last name. In fact, "Wynn-Winn" is my family reunion's signature logo. The spelling of our last name *W-y-n-n* was passed down to us for several generations. However, we found out, that in 1904, my great-great grandfather William's last name was spelled *W-i-n-n* instead. History tells the story that one of William Winn's children, Albert Winn, who was my great-grandfather, was born into slavery, and his birth record showed his last name spelled as *W-i-n-n*. But later in the 1900's, Albert's youngest son John, my grandfather, changed the spelling of his last name to W-y-n-n, like his older siblings, during a time when slavery gave way to sharecropping. Either way, the spelling of *Wynn or Winn,* gives me a reason to Just Win. So, I gratefully accepted my "Wynn-Winn" situation.

People who strongly believe in winning usually find a way to succeed. My Uncle Larry, who has received three kidney transplants and has other medical issues, is living proof of what a winner is. Larry, who played football and is an avid football fan, relates his victories in football metaphors, such as, "It's the fourth quarter of the game, third down and inches to go for a touchdown. Time to change the game." I recited this metaphor to him during one of his kidney transplants while he was in intensive care. Once he recovered, he continued to speak positively about his next win over an operation or an intense procedure to relieve some pain, rather than complaining about his health issues and limitations. His winning attitude and spirit led him to take on countless hours of researching our family history with pleasure. Uncle Larry has such an extraordinary attitude about being a winner, his energy and effort encourages our entire family to be winners, as well.

"Winning isn't everything but wanting to win is."

~ Vince Lombardi

Winning Goals Elevate Success

Your future is created by what you do today, not tomorrow, so it is important for winners to have winning goals. Make goals to elevate success so that the action you create will give you the results you want. Winners are people who attack life with a plan to get a big win, like earning that desired job they applied for. They accept and appreciate small wins, like finding the connection that leads them to getting that desired job.

Former Detroit Lion's football star, Barry Sanders had a winning spirit based on his goals to succeed. "Let's just win it and go home," was one of his driving goals. Barry Sanders was a true asset to the Detroit Lions and a true testament to winning, with playing abilities that afforded him to set many team and National Football League records.

Winning goals should be:

- *Specific*, clear, and defined to win. Write down how you plan to meet a specific goal. This plan should give a precise, clear picture of what you will do to get the win.
- *Measurable*, so that you can determine progress by evaluating the time needed to succeed. You should use precise numbers to measure your degree of success.
- *Attainable*, achievable, and possible to complete. Winning goals should not be set without the possibility of achieving them.
- *Set* for a deadline. Time restrictions are critical because you must decide when you have reached your goal(s) based on a timeline.

- *Relevant.* A pertinent goal will give you the necessary direction to achieve what you want and to understand why it is important to you.

To elevate your winning goals, you must always have a positive attitude with the drive and determination to take the necessary actions to achieve your goals.

No Excuses, No Blame

The Just Win habit is a survival kit for winning because circumstances, obstacles, or your environment can't get in the way of your win. No matter what comes your way, you should never give up. Often, we make excuses, blaming a situation or other people, in order to give up. Not to say that unexpected or uncontrollable situations don't exist, because I have had my share. However, when a goal is truly important to you, there should be no excuse to approach your goal with uncertainty or a lack of conviction.

When dealing with my depression, I made excuses for myself for why I did not want to get well because I was in a comfort zone with my disorder. I did not always tell my doctor or therapist what was really going on. This deception may have been because I was afraid of getting well, or that the trust level I had with my physicians did not meet my expectations. I had to learn to set my goals in easy-to-accomplish steps, to avoid any excuse for achieving them.

Stop making excuses that prevent you from moving toward achieving your goals with a positive attitude, whether it's about your career, losing weight, or overcoming obstacles and fear. With the Just Win habit, I learned how to keep my winning attitude by not allowing myself to make excuses or blame others. Just Win!

Coach "Win" Action Steps:

Develop a strong "Win-Win" mission statement that can be used in any situation:

Write down at least 5 steps, small or big, that define your "Win-Win" situation.

Chapter 10: Habit Six: Just Win

To have winning goals that elevate your success, you must determine why these goals are important to your success. List the goals that will identify your success:

"A repeat is just another opportunity to Win."

~Michael Wynn

Habit Seven: "Think Repeat"

Habits Come With Practice

During my journey, after finding the reasons to move forward, it still took me some time to readjust my life because of my scattered thinking and mood swings. I visualized my faith that came with following actions from the Think Repeat habit, which shows the importance of repetition by doing something over for the second time to gain more clarity and become more focused. The information that is gathered to overcome an obstacle the first time will give you guidance to win for the second time. This habit gave me a stronger mindset to practice the other routines that seemed to work for my overcoming my disorder. When you make a commitment to practice wise habits, you essentially maximize the impact of your training and the improvement that you seek.

Sometimes you need to embrace the discomfort that comes with growing and improving. If you do not practice the things you have to do, then you may not grow beyond the limited space where you are at your present time. Experiencing discomfort, however, will make you think about moving out of the space that makes you feel that way. You move towards improvement because of the mere fact that you want to move forward to be free from the discomfort.

This concept of discomfort reminds me about Coach Dozier, my high-school football coach, who expected you to practice like you were playing a real game, or you experienced his discomfort. Coach Dozier publicly praised a player when he did well during practice. If someone didn't do a play correctly, he spoke directly to the player by calling him out on his failed attempt, wrong technique, or incomplete process. But, when he just stood there in silence with a disappointed nod of the head or just turned away, you never knew what was coming next, and you had to raise your level of practice to achieve his confidence again. The discomfort caused simply by Coach Dozier's silence encouraged you to improve your game.

The Think Repeat habit positioned me to practice harder and gain self-confidence to achieve my goals for recovery. The Think Repeat habit made me consider the challenges I faced the first time, only to encourage me to practice harder and gain better results. It did not take long for me to develop enough confidence to welcome obstacles, barriers, and setbacks and to see them as opportunities to move forward.

"It only takes one reason to move forward."

~ Lisa Nichols

Chapter 11: Habit Seven: Think Repeat

Journaling Results Are for a Replay

The habit of journaling my daily thoughts or logging information about the good and bad things that went on in my life played a critical part in my recovery. This information was the key for me to follow and track my progress.

During my treatments, I found out a lot about myself. I journaled the side effects of my mood swings, like my happy and sad days, my positive and negative thoughts, my sugar addiction when I was sensitive to sugar, my desire to work out seven days a week with little sleep, my outbursts when something did not go right, or my terrible spending habits.

As I reinvented myself, the Think Repeat habit was important to follow because I could look back on my performance and the actions I took. Reviewing the information that was gathered was useful in determining how I described my day. The information I journaled gave me an understanding of what I needed to do to improve. The Think Repeat habit to journal certain situations, moods, or what you feed your body could be the source of information that is necessary to avoid certain objects or situations when moving forward.

I still journal my daily thoughts and log information, as I find it necessary for comparison with other journaled information. Often times, we cannot see the significance of an event or the importance of the lesson until we compare the results of our actions. When you know exactly what you want and what you need to fix, journaling daily information, like how to fill your day with happiness, how to get organized, your good or bad habits, or steps to get out of debt, is necessary.

I start my daily journal in the morning and write throughout the day, collecting important information like:

- The time I wake up
- The amount of sleep I got
- My blood pressure in the morning and evening
- My objectives for the day
- My mood through the day
- What I read during the day
- My end statement for my day
- A praise to give to myself

During my morning yoga exercises, and meditation, I think through the intentions and objectives that I want for the day, which I then write in my journal. Sometimes, daily journaling may become a problem because you may lose the daily motivation and the effort that is necessary. However, you must find a way to motivate yourself by making the impossible necessary. Tell yourself that you must start big to finish big; don't wait, decide; and don't quit, go harder for the win!

"People often say motivation doesn't last. Well, neither does bathing – that's why we recommend it daily."

~Zig Ziglar

Redo, Readjust, and Rejoice

To overcome any obstacle, you must pay attention to the long-term solution, not just the short-term. Because of my disorder, I often tried to look for an easy, short-term solution. But, I had to ask myself, "Should I try a quick fix and take the heavy doses of medication?" Or, "Should I learn how to change my personal behavior with therapy so that I can resolve my disorder?"

Because I didn't want to be reliant on medication, I finally embraced a long-term solution to get well. The results that you compile for a replay may be the playbook for your next win.

1. Are you willing to get the necessary results? It is necessary to focus on the results you want in order to move in a direction to win. You must allow yourself the freedom to act and think about the results that are needed to become a master in your craft.

2. Are you committed to practice? Sometimes you have to have an attitude of never being satisfied. Be willing to practice over again and make the adjustments to achieve your goals.

3. Can you count on yourself? You must be true to yourself and always be in control. When you Visualize Faith, you rejoice in your victory because you can see the win. Continue to have self-respect for yourself and don't be motivated by money or any other worldly material to manipulate or alter your thinking.

4. Are you curious about winning again? Confidence is your greatest asset; however, confidence doesn't always get the win. Energy and persistence will give you the power to conquer your obstacles for a win. But sometimes, you must Think Repeat and find the right strategy to get the win.

To want and to honor the end process sometimes means you have to redo the things that are not working, readjust to change the environment or situation, and then rejoice in a victory that will come for the second time!

"When you reach the top, keep climbing."

~Zen Aphorism

Coach "Win" Action Steps:

"Practice Makes Perfect" is a phrase used to convey the regular exercise of an activity or skill to become proficient in it. What is your practice mission? *Write a Mission Statement for your practice:*

Write down at least 5 areas that you feel are important for daily journaling:

Habits Don't Lie

Logging comparative information allows you to see the percentage of money or effort spent on an activity over a period of time. This information could be helpful for comparing data, like money invested monthly, your spending habits, physical conditioning time, or the time you spend on social media. Details are necessary for you to make a comparison and recognize growth. *Write down at least 5 areas that you are committed to logging in your journal daily.*:

Conclusion

Demonstrate Your Win!

Wow, what a journey! Looking back over my life was my way of moving through my journey to understand how to use my habits. Throughout this book, I wanted to share with you how to overcome obstacles to win by using habits. As a habit success coach, I express to my clients that, "Habits will determine your level of success," and in this book I gave many reasons why. By looking back on each of the habits, you will be able to achieve a breakthrough and elevate your success. So, let's briefly review the seven habits that you can use to achieve your win.

VISUALIZE FAITH

The Visualize Faith habit shows how daily prayer and meditation can bring you freedom and mental relaxation, once you let go of your grudges and emotions. Daily affirmations will support and confirm your willingness to conquer fear and become unstoppable. This habit will also guide you through a transformation, from requiring physical pictures of expressions and memories, to allowing the memories to live on by visualizing past moments without the physical substance.

BE REAL

The Be Real habit is a practical approach for living an authentic life on a daily routine. Through this process you can use your authentic voice with integrity, motivation, and inspiration which will allow you to shine and be noticed by others. This habit will help you to be consistent as you make peace, forgive, love, and go forward with no regrets.

TARGET SUCCESS

The Target Success habit helps you identify your audience and the areas of focus for your purpose, passion, and accountability. This habit will also allow you to find greatness through personal development and create a driving desire to achieve your goals and objectives with energy, using a process of working smarter and not harder. Through improved connections with relationships, you will be able to evaluate and bring success to immense fulfillment.

KNOW MONEY

The Know Money habit redefines the importance of financial literacy as a life mission for you. Regardless of your knowledge of money, it is essential to exercise daily habits when it comes to managing money. This habit will provide you the energy to transform your relationship with money by having a goal to create ways to achieve financial independence and to receive your abundance. The Know Money habit will challenge you through bankruptcy recovery to a "Fresh Start" and bring awareness to building a system for controlling spending. The habit will also express the use of growth plans for multiple streams of income and recognize the importance of a financial-net wellness plan to develop a living legacy.

LIVE HEALTH

The Live Health habit provides the health awareness for understanding your mind and body. This daily habit gives you guidelines for good nutrition, physical activity, stress-coping methods, positive relationships, and career choices for healthy living. The Live Health habit also encourages health-wellness and fitness-obedience with your health specialist.

JUST WIN

The Just Win habit assists you in focusing on your daily passion to win and visualizing an environment free from toxins, chaos, and negativity. The Just Win habit gives praise to small wins, the same way you celebrate a big win. It creates a spirit to receive "Win-Win" situations that are inevitable, with winning goals that are specific, measurable, attainable, timely, and relevant. The Just Win habit will get you on a daily track to think positively and surround yourself with the right people who have the right attitude to win, with no excuses and no blame. Just Win!

THINK REPEAT

The Think Repeat habit allows you to have a do-over. Habits come with practice, and the importance of repetition by doing something over for the second time will help you gain more clarity and become more focused. A daily habit of journaling your thoughts and logging certain situations, moods, attitudes, or what you eat will help you improve, while avoiding negative things. You will learn to honor the end process that allows you to redo what is not working, readjust by changing the environment or situation, and then rejoice by demonstrating your win!

I encourage you to follow these habits daily in order to improve, have peace, happiness, and winning success in your life. As your Habit Success Coach, I will help you optimize your daily performance, prepare you for a financial and health wellness plan as you overcome obstacles.

About the Author

Michael D. Wynn is President of Coach "Win," LLC, and a habit success coach, speaker, trainer, and author from Detroit, Michigan. As a certified Authenticity Coach, Financial Literacy Trainer, and Fraud Examiner, Michael coaches and speaks on subjects like personal and professional development, financial literacy, and health fitness. His services provide support for optimizing daily performance, growing and protecting businesses, and managing stress with a Habit Matrix. He uses his authentic voice as he gives thought-provoking, entertaining, and motivational support to his audience.

Michael was also a proud recipient of the 2006 Outstanding Financial Literacy Award from the Michigan Accounting Aid Society. Michael enjoys reading, watching sports, yoga, weight training, going on walks and traveling around the world with his wife Joyce. Michael is also grateful for the time and value of spending time with his children, grandchildren and family.
To see more on the author, and for speaking engagements and book signings go to: www.michaelwynn.com

After reading this book you should have gained enough reasons why you should continue on a path of habits to overcome obstacles and to claim your breakthrough and to win! Please go to: www.coachwin.com to find out more about coaching, speaking, and training services, and offers for your personal development.

Follow Michael on Social Media:
https://www.facebook.com/michelwynnLive/

Follow him on Instagram @coachmikewins

Twitter @michaelwynnLive
Email him at mikewynn@coachwin.com

Made in the USA
Middletown, DE
02 September 2018